Ghost Towns of Wyoming

Ghost Towns of Wyoming

By
Donald C. Miller

PRUETT PUBLISHING COMPANY
Boulder, Colorado

© 1977 by Donald C. Miller

All rights reserved, including those to reproduce this book, or parts thereof, in any form without permission in writing from the Publisher.

Library of Congress Cataloging in Publication Data

Miller, Donald C   1933-
  Ghost towns of Wyoming.

  Includes bibliographical references and index.
  1. Wyoming — Description and Travel — 1951-
2. Cities and towns, Ruined, extinct, etc. — Wyoming.
I. Title.
F765.M54   978.7'03   77-22097
ISBN 0-87108-511-9

Paperback Edition, First Printing: 1982
ISBN; 0-87108-616-6

2 3 4 5 6 7 8 9

Printed in the United States of America

All photographs by Don Miller unless otherwise acknowledged.

Foreword

Rodman W. Paul, in *Mining Frontiers of the Far West*, wrote, "Wyoming itself was not important in mining. A considerable 'excitement' over gold near South Pass, the historic route through the Rockies, burgeoned briefly in 1867-1868, just as the Union Pacific Railroad was being built; but it soon collapsed, leaving behind its empty 'cities' and little groups of miners working their isolated claims."[1]

Yet, this volume includes accounts of about 100 Wyoming "ghost towns" that began as mining camps.

Mining, especially for coal, was more prevalent in Wyoming than Paul and others recognize. According to the U.S. Bureau of Mines in *Analysis of Wyoming Coals* (1927), "The coal reserves of Wyoming are sufficient to supply present market demands for 50,000 years to come . . . and exceed by more than seventy times all coal mined within the United States in the 115-year period between 1807 and 1921."

About 1880 a perceptive Englishman named William A. Baillie-Grohman roamed the wilds of what was to become Wyoming. His remarks seem appropriate. He wrote: "Ruins are, however, not necessarily the result of age. Nowhere does the traveller come across so many signs of deplorable decay as just in the West. He can see entire 'cities' erected a few years back, and inhabited by several thousands of eager miners, totally deserted and slowly crumbling to ruin, the playthings of gales and dry rot."

Another observer noted something of the people who inhabited mining camps—in this case, South Pass City. "A certain class of people cannot content themselves to remain in any community beyond the time when the newness of things has worn off. This class kept hearing of new and rich fields in Idaho, Montana, and Nevada, and of course it was their nature to give up everything and go. They were the rolling stones . . . and whether they gathered moss at other places it is impossible to say."[2]

As elsewhere, miners in Wyoming used picks, shovels, pans, arrastres, long toms, hydraulic giants, blasting powder, and sluice boxes to help scratch out precious metals. One enterprising individual even used geese to gather his gold. The Laramie *Republican*[3] gave this account of gold seeking: "H. F. Williams, who owns a ranch near this place, is watching a flock of geese in their daily wanderings, and is prospecting wherever they feed in the hope that he will discover a deposit of gold of fabulous richness.

"Recently Williams killed a goose and in its crop discovered a score of particles of gold. He killed five other geese and in the crop of each found gold, securing all together seventy specks of the metal worth $1.05.

"Since then he has been watching the geese [as] they feed, expecting to locate the spot from which the gold came. Inasmuch as the fowls have the run of a large field, cut by several dry ravines, the search is not simple and has involved much labor which has been fruitless.

"Eventually, however, Williams expects to locate the placer deposits from which the gold came."

And now, roughly a century later, much of the mining frontier can still be seen or sensed through familiarity with its colorful past.

An understanding of these mining camps is important, for as Charles Shinn wrote in his classic book *Mining Camps: A Study in American Frontier Government*, ". . . over the western third of the United States, institutional life traces its beginnings to the mining camp: that is the original contribution of the American pioneer to the art of self-government."

Additionally, armchair or on-site "ghost town hunting" can be one hell of a lot of fun!

Ghost Towns of Wyoming

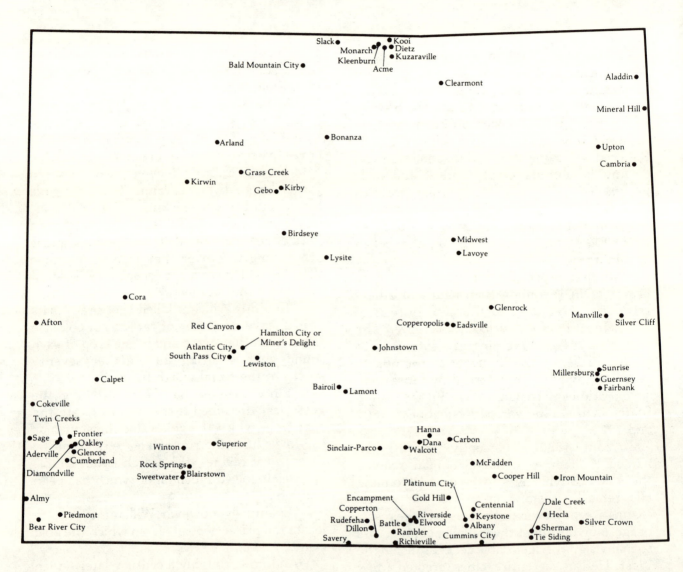

Details about the history of **Aderville**, near present-day Kemmerer, are sketchy.

The settlement was founded in the 1870s, and for a time was the center of a mining area. However, when coal deposits were discovered at Kemmerer, the residents of Aderville moved to that community.

At one time Aderville was the home of saloon keeper-soul keeper "Preachin' Lime Huggins," who, like the rest of the townspeople, eventually moved to Kemmerer. Huggins is remembered for his advice, "Don't influence a man already under the influence."[4]

Although **Afton** was not necessarily founded as a mining camp, mines were located nearby, including the Vail (or Star Valley) in which five miners lost their lives in an explosion on February 11, 1938.

Gold, silver, and copper were extracted from the area. The still-existing town rests in Star Valley on the Salt River.

At one time Afton sported a church valued at $50,000, a schoolhouse which cost $6,000 to build, and a daily stage that connected with the Oregon Short Line Railroad at Montpelier, Idaho.

The State Board of Immigration[5] reported that at one time a creamery in Afton paid between $10,000 and $15,000 monthly to area dairy farmers.

Concrete steps leading nowhere near Afton

Afton, featuring the world's largest elkhorn arch

The small town of **Aladdin** still survives in northeastern Crook County.

The town was probably named for the daughter of Aladdin Hicks, promoter of the Aladdin coal mines.[6]

The settlement had "railroad communication" with Belle Fourche, South Dakota, through the Wyoming and Missouri Valley Railroad, and the State Board of Immigration prophesized, "Its coal deposits insure a permanent growth for the town."[7]

The prediction proved false. In 1920 the population was twenty. In 1970 it was ten.

Barret Town was west of Aladdin, while **Baker Town** lay to the east; both were coal mining towns on the Wyoming and Missouri River Railroad.

Alamo consisted of a post office and ferry station operated by a Mr. Shaffer, native of Texas, who gave the town its name.

Tacetta B. Walker, in *Stories of Early Days in Wyoming*,[8] recounts this story about Shaffer's ferry: "His ferry was not a large one and one day an outfit coming along insisted on crossing the whole thing at once. Shaffer did not want them to as he said the ferry was not strong enough, but they loaded teams and wagon on regardless and sank the whole thing, ferry, teams, and wagon in the middle of the Big Horn [River]. After that passengers had to be rowed across in a small boat."

Almy began as a coal town—probably in 1869—on a branch of the Union Pacific about one-half dozen miles north of Evanston. The town most likely received its name for coalminer-discoverer T. J. Almy, an early-day supervisor for the Rocky Mountain Coal Company, which produced coal for the Central Pacific Railroad in the area.

Almy was rich in coal deposits. It was also rich in high explosive gas and coal dust which killed at least fifty-one men and boys by explosion and fire in 1881 and 1886.[9]

Almy was plagued by labor disputes and endured what has been called "thirty-two years of unhappy operations." The statement is possibly false, since mining occurred longer than that—for thirty-six years[10]—and all of them apparently unhappy years.

In 1870 hundreds of Chinese were imported as low-wage, nonunion miners. It has been estimated that at one time Chinese miners outnumbered whites by 600 to 20.[11] Racial sores festered, and during a race riot in 1885 troops were called from Fort Bridger.[12]

Finally, in 1906, mining ceased because it cost one dollar to mine each ton of coal.[13]

Many Almy structures were moved to Spring Valley and Cumberland.

Almy remains a sleepy little town on Highway 89, possessing few physical reminders of its mining heyday.

Arland's life was short. It was founded by Messrs. Corbett and Arland and in 1884 consisted of a store, a hotel, a saloon, and a post office. In 1896 the buildings were moved to Meeteetse, and the town disappeared.

Atlantic City was founded in 1868 about four miles from South Pass City. Some say it was so named because the residents believed that water from the town ran to the Atlantic Ocean.[14]

By 1869 the population had reached about 2,000, and Atlantic City proudly proclaimed that it had the territory's first brewery.

In 1878, when South Pass was almost deserted, seven stamp mills still hammered away at Atlantic City.

In 1884[15] Frenchman Emile Granier decided to build hydraulic pipes to wash the gravels along Rock Creek. Disaster after disaster befell his project, however, and Granier was forced to dispose of it. He returned to France penniless, to spend his remaining days in a debtor's prison.

A thirty-stamp mill was built in close proximity to the Mammoth Lode, near Atlantic City, by Colonel Elliott. The mine was salted.[16]

Indian depredations were common in the area, and the frightened citizens asked that a fort be built. In 1870 the army built Camp Stambaugh north of Atlantic City and garrisoned it with two companies of infantry. Eight years later the post was abandoned; there was no one left to protect.

Shortly after the turn of the century some mining took place in the Atlantic City area, and in the 1930s dredging operations were carried on.

Muriel Sibell Wolle writes an interesting account of the camp's first postmaster—

Robert McAuley, who went to Atlantic City in 1869 and lived there for twenty-nine years. She reports: "During that time he lived in three counties, two territories, and one state; yet he never moved his residence or business. When he arrived, Atlantic City was in Dakota Territory. A month or two later, on April 15, 1869, the area, which had been designated Wyoming Territory in July 1868, was formally recognized, and J. A. Campbell was inaugurated as its first governor. Carter County, as set up by the miners, had been recognized by the Dakota legislature in 1867. In 1869 its name was changed to Sweetwater. In 1884, by a rearrangement of boundaries, Atlantic City and the adjacent towns fell within newly created Fremont County. The Territory of Wyoming became a state in 1890."[17]

The Atlantic City mine still operates, producing taconite. Recently the townsite was bought by a mining company, and the land was subdivided.

Atlantic City—*Western History Research Center, University of Wyoming*

Atlantic City—*Wyoming State Archives and Historical Department*

The hotel at Atlantic City

An overview of Atlantic City as it appeared in 1974

The Episcopal Church at Atlantic City. Services are held during July and August.

7

Bairoil was named for Charles Bair, a prominent sheep raiser from Billings, Montana. Bair financed and promoted the first oil development in the district.

The first oil rig used in the Bairoil area was hauled in by a horse team in 1916.

Today Bairoil is a fairly flourishing town, boasting a population of about 300.

High in the Bighorn Mountains near the mysterious Indian Medicine Wheel, a settlement known as **Bald Mountain City** grew up.

Originally prospectors worked the ground for the flour gold, but later the individual claims were sold to mining companies, one of which was formed by eastern capital to work the "Fortunatus" lode.

Initially the settlement may have been named Fortunatus, but it later was called a variety of names, including Baldy City, Old Baldy, Old Gold City, City of Broken Hearts, and Bald Mountain City. It is also possible that Fortunatus was a separate city, located one mile from Bald Mountain City.[18]

The company that bought the Fortunatus lode purchased a monster amalgamator powered by three engines. It took twenty-four bull teams to get the mining machinery up the approximate sixty-five-mile trail to Bald Mountain City. It is reported that on occasion along the treacherous trail the oxen in the center of the string would be hoisted off the ground by the draw line.[19]

The company spent from an estimated one-half million to two million dollars,[20] but operations proved unsuccessful in this high country where the men could work only three months of the year. The amalgamator was dismantled, its scoops later used for irrigation purposes.

One man stayed on after the others had left Bald Mountain City. He had come to strike it rich and then return East to marry. The sole survivor of Bald Mountain silently prospected the niggardly gravels. One day his concerned parents and sweetheart found him, demented, in his cabin. He apparently did not recognize them and yelled that they would not steal his gold. But the gravel he had collected was just that and not rich placer deposits. As a result of the unhappy incidents, Bald Mountain City has been called "The City of Broken Hearts."

It is silent and usually cold at the scattered, tattered remains of Bald Mountain City, and the site seems diminished by the towering nearby peaks of Medicine Mountain and Bald Mountain, 9,956 and 10,041 feet high, respectively.

Searching for gold at Bald Mountain City—
Western History Research Center, University of Wyoming

The sparse remains of Bald Mountain City

The town of **Battle** was built on the site of the Battle Mountain massacre and may have received its name from the incident.[21]

As well as being a mining center, Battle was a stopover point for freighters headed westward.

Copper mining probably began in the area in 1879, but it was not until 1898 that Battle was platted. At one time the settlement included five saloons, a newspaper, an assay office, a town hall, four general stores, a stable, a men's apparel shop, a dry goods emporium, a mercantile, and a school.

The story goes that the local whores would complain about the Mexican shepherds who worked in the area. The herders apparently left sheep ticks in the "funhouse" beds.[22]

Since Battle rested on land originally used for grazing, the sheepherders and miners clashed frequently. One of the more serious encounters happened in Smyzer's saloon. It was precipitated by gunman Kid Blizzard, but exactly what happened is not known. In one verison [23] of the story, sheepherders began to curse Blizzard while he was tending bar. He retaliated by striking a herder over the head with his gun. A fight ensued, and the next morning one herder was found dead behind the schoolhouse. Another account relates that

Battle—*Western History Research Center, University of Wyoming*

Kid Blizzard started a fight, and that although some Mexicans were killed, the inquest determined that they died "from causes unknown."[24]

At least one devastating fire ravaged Battle. In its July 20, 1899 edition, the Platte Valley *Lyre* reported that the town had been built during the winter while the snow was deep. The residents had cut off trees at snow level to build cabins. When the spring thaws came, Battleites found the town streets full of stumps several feet high. The townspeople burned the stumps, but they also burned a good share of their new settlement. The newspaper commented: "It is probable that Battleites will grub their stumps out hereafter."

Battle was abandoned in 1907. In 1933 CCC workers demolished what remained of the town and established a campground. Shafts, dumps, a cemetery containing thirteen bodies, and a United States Forest Service marker are all that remain of Battle, whose corporate existence extended only from 1898 to 1907.

The Battle townsite

A homemade marker shows where Jim Johnson is buried at Battle.

Bear River City (Beartown) is generally considered to have been a transportation and trade center, but coal mining also occurred in the area.

The settlement—originally called Gilmer—was founded in 1867 before the Union Pacific tracklayers arrived. The railroad construction gangs came in October 1868, accompanied by many camp followers and outspoken newspaper editor Legh Freeman. Freeman vehemently attacked the rowdy elements associated with the tracklaying crews. The editorial columns of his *Frontier Index* were full of tirades against these "seedy" individuals. Partly through Freeman's urging, a committee of vigilance was formed to provide protection against the roughs.

The special targets of the vigilantes were three desperadoes—Little Jack O'Neil, Jimmy Reed, and Jimmy Powers. The three were strung up one night and left hanging near the railroad tracks.

Word got around that Legh Freeman had organized the hangings. Freeman denied the accusation and said that another man—Charles Stebbins—was the culprit.

Rowdies who thought the hanged trio had been wronged were rounded up by the vigilantes and held in the newly constructed log jail. The next morning about 300 sympathizers of the jailed men came to get them. They shot the marshal, tore down the jail house door, and released the prisoners. They also decided to hang editor Freeman, but the newspaperman was warned and managed to slip away. However, his newspaper office was destroyed.[25]

The stage was set for a battle between the townspeople and the rowdies.

The armed battle raged all day.

Finally, a town resident[26] managed to reach Fort Bridger on horseback to summon the troops. They were not needed, however, for that night the roughs headed for the hills.

As the railroad pushed farther west, Bear River City lost its population. Today it is gone.

Bear River City (photograph taken about 1868) was along the Union Pacific Railroad. The town vanished within a few months after the track crew moved on.—*Union Pacific Railroad Museum Collection*

Blairstown was founded by Scotsmen Archie and Duncan Blair, who opened a coal seam in the area, employed miners, and built a three-room dwelling complete with restaurant.

This was perhaps the first privately owned and operated coal mine in Wyoming.[27] It was established in 1886.

Most of the early inhabitants were housed in dugouts along the bank of Bitter Creek.

Until 1888 it was necessary to run a daily water train to Blairstown from Green River—at a cost of twenty-five cents a barrel. Later a pipeline was constructed between the two towns.

Not long after Blairstown's founding the Union Pacific found extensive outcroppings of coal near the town, and the Rock Springs mines were subsequently opened. A result of the 1875 strike was the moving of Blairstown's railroad station; and most of the miners moved with it.

A few residents stubbornly lived on at Blairstown, but in 1926 all homes in the settlement were removed from the creek banks and Blairstown ceased to exist.

Birdseye was a mining camp on the stage route between Shoshoni and Thermopolis. Little is known of this short-lived camp.

Bonanza was located northeast of Worland in 1887. Probably as early as 1884 people in the area noticed oil oozing to the surface. It was easy to dig up and use for a variety of purposes, and its quality reportedly was so high that the oil could be burned in lamps without refining.

Bonanza became the headquarters for the Bonanza oil fields.

The *Big Horn Rustler*, first published by Tom Dagget in 1889[28], forecast a bright future for Bonanza; but the town had a short life. The oil companies left in 1890, and at last report, a single log structure was all that remained of the misnamed town.

Calpet was established northeast of Kemmerer by the California Petroleum Company. It was an oil field camp.

Cambria, believed by some to have been the West's only anthracite coal-producing town,[29] was founded in 1889[30] but was not incorporated under the general laws of Wyoming until after the 1910 census. The mine's output was used to fire Burlington Railroad trains. Some salt was also mined in the area.

How Cambria received its name is controversial. The authors of one book state, "Some old-timers, now moved to other places, live to tongue-roll the name Cambria. With nostalgia they recall back when their real blood princess was born, a little blue-eyed babe of a traveling show manager's wife. 'Cambria' she was christened in the miners' interpretation of a royal coronation."[31] Another source says, "Cambria is a Latin name for the English province of mountainous Wales, a great coal-producing country."[32]

Cambria was a company town,[33] and Cambria miners lived in a bunkhouse (called the "Bull Pen") built by the company (Kirkpatrick Brothers & Collins). The basement had a gymnasium and dance hall which served as an entertainment center for the miners. But no saloon tempted Cambria's hundreds[34] of thirsty miners because the bosses opposed liquor. Instead, beer and liquor wagons plied the road from neighboring Newcastle, providing Cambria with a sort of mobile saloon service.

Between twelve and thirteen million tons of coal were shipped from the Cambria mines. Much of it was converted to coke by ovens[35] and shipped to the Homestake gold mine in Lead, South Dakota.

The Right Reverend Ethelbert Talbot had an experience with a Cambria miner which he related in his book *My People of the Plains*.[36] He writes: "I had held service and preached the night before in our new church at Cambria, Wyoming, where a large number of Italians were employed in the coal-mines. Early the next morning I took the train for New Castle, a few miles down the canon. Soon after I took my seat a young Italian entered. He had evidently been in our country but a short time, and his only associates had probably been miners, whose language was not always most chaste. He quite suprised me when he recognized me and said:

" 'Ah, you ze cardinal. I hear you talk last night. Damn pretty church! Damn big crowd! Damn good talk.' "

Cambria became the "melting pot" for an

estimated twenty-three nationalities.³⁷

Cambria is one of the few western mining towns suspected of being under the influence of "the mafia." The Black Hand, reportedly a branch of the mafia, infiltrated the town and terrorized it. The unsubstantiated story is that the murders of Giacchino, a bartender (and possibly bootlegger) from Newcastle, and his driver, Peter Nora, were caused by the Black Hand. Vigilantes were formed and apparently took care of the problem.

The schoolhouse was on a hill above town. Three hundred and sixty-five steps (perhaps 600) led to it. About forty dwellings were situated on the same hill (actually located in South Dakota), which became known as "Antelope City."

The veins pinched out, and mining ceased March 15, 1928. That same year the town was abandoned. Cambria now squats on private land, and guests from the Flying-V dude ranch are generally the only visitors to this once lively "plaything of the wind."

Cambria coal camp—*Stimson Photo Collection, Wyoming State Archives & Historical Department*

The Cambria Concert Band—*Western History Research Center, University of Wyoming*

This part of Cambria was in Wyoming. The residential part of the settlement was several hundred wooden steps away, in Antelope City, South Dakota.

Carbon about 1875—*Union Pacific Railroad Museum Collection*

Carbon, founded in 1868, was Wyoming's first coal town and the first mining camp to be established by the Union Pacific.[38]

Carbon is generally considered to have been sired by Thomas Wardell, who leased Union Pacific lands at Carbon for a period of fifteen years. He contracted to sell coal for six dollars per ton for the first two years, five dollars a ton for the next three, four dollars per ton for the next four, and three dollars a ton for the next six years. Later, the Union Pacific took over the mines.

Seven[39] mines were opened at Carbon, and during its heyday 600 men were employed there. They may have taken out as much as 200 tons of coal each day.[40]

Early-day Carbon has been described as resembling a prairie dog village: "Reclining against the sage slopes, the stovepipes bobbed upward and outward like inquisitive gopher heads. The shoddies in which the miners lived were fashioned of stone slab gathered from nearby knolls, or of twelve-foot boards bought by the railroad and used upright, chinked with sod and roofed with mortared earth or flattened tin cans."[41]

The area around Carbon had long been Indian hunting ground, and hostilities frequently broke out between miners and Indians. During those times it was not uncommon for Carbon's women and children to stay in the mines at night, while guards kept "Injun watch" on the surface.

Troubles broke out in the mines, too. In 1874 four men were killed by cave-ins. That year also saw the burning of the No. 1 mine shaft and the entrapment of mules Sage and Pete. The miners were not about to give up on the mules, and with the aid of rope and windlass, one man went down the shaft and secured ropes around the animals. Sage was hoisted to the surface without incident, but

feisty Pete began to struggle half way up the shaft, and the rope slipped around his neck. When he reached the surface he seemed to be dead. He revived, however, and went back to work, along with Sage, pulling coal cars through the mine tunnels.

Shortly after Sage and Pete had been hauled up the No. 1 shaft, an Italian was hired to fill in the mine. When he was about midway through the job, he fell down the shaft and was killed. Another incident occurred in the No. 1 mine when the shaft was being flooded by water entering through surface caves. The women of the town sewed together sacking, to be filled with sand and used as levees for diverting the water flow away from the mine.[42]

No. 2 mine had an interesting ventilation system. Boys called "trappers" would pull strings which opened and shut doors to the mine tunnels. The door facing the prevailing wind was opened, and fresh air was forced through the mine.

While young boys operated the ventilation system, older boys were used as "spraggers." Two "sprags"[43]—pointed wooden poles about one dozen inches in length—were shoved by "spraggers" into the spokes of the ore cars. This would decelerate the cars as gravity sped them toward the mine entrance. Other boys were stationed along the path to pull out the sprags when the ore cars needed to pick up speed. This alternate slowing down and speeding up of the ore cars demanded skill, and spragging was considered a dangerous occupation. Finger losses were common among spraggers.

Nor were life and limb necessarily safe above ground in Carbon. In June 1878 Dutch Charlie Burris, Big Nose George Parrot, and others tried to rob a Union Pacific train.[44] They were pursued by deputies Robert Widdowfield, Tip Vincent, and others. The two deputies were shot to death while examining a still-warm campfire built by the desperadoes. The outlaws made their getaway, but Dutch Charlie was later caught in Montana. He was scheduled for extradition to Rawlins via the Union Pacific, but on the night of January 23, 1879, when the train he was riding stopped on schedule at Carbon, a grim group of men took him off and hanged him from a telegraph pole crossbeam.[45]

Calamity Jane is supposed to have spent some time in Carbon in order to visit her lover, Bill Steers.

At least four churches were built in Carbon; one of them blew down three times before it was finally completed.

Carbon was crippled by a fire that swept through much of the business district on June 19, 1890. But Carbon was rebuilt and grew to rival nearby Cheyenne. Following the fire, Mayor John Lewis required all buildings to have brick chimneys and insulated stovepipes. Mayor Lewis also ordered the building of a water tower (the town's only source of water had previously been a cistern) near abandoned No. 5 mine.

Labor troubles and lawsuits crippled the Union Pacific's ability to profitably produce coal, and by 1899 most of the coal was gone. The U.P. opened a new mine in the area that year, but mining ceased in 1902. Most of the miners were then ordered to the newly opened mines near Hanna.

The Carbon State Bank had been organized December 9, 1891, with a capital stock of $15,000. When Carbon was deserted, the bank was moved to Hanna, and its name was changed to the Hanna National Bank (it was later to become a state bank). This enterprise is the oldest state bank in Wyoming.[46]

Still, Carbon did not die immediately. For a brief period it served as the Wyoming headquarters of the Denver, Laramie, and Northwestern Railroad and had a population of 117 early in the twentieth century.[47]

Today only ruins and a cemetery mark the site.

DUGOUTS AND LOG HOUSES OF CARBON IN 1876

Carbon—*Western History Research Center, University of Wyoming*

The unusual grave marker of Henniette Grabenhorst in the Carbon cemetery

The marker of Nils Simelius in the Carbon cemetery attests to the many nationalities at work in the Carbon mines.

This area is thought to be the site of the mass burial of miners burned beyond recognition in a Carbon mine disaster.

Most of original **Centennial** is gone, replaced by modern structures. However, a couple of older buildings are a reminder of the days when Centennial was the site of four gold mines.

Centennial was founded in 1876.[48] In addition to being a mining town, it was a trading center for ranches in the Centennial Valley.

Colonel Stephen W. Downey is said to have refused $100,000[49] for a rich gold lode he uncovered on the edge of the Medicine Bow mountains.

The mines gave out, and an attempt by promoters to revive a gold rush in 1892 failed. Nevertheless, during warm weather area residents can still be found searching for "colors."

The depot at Centennial

Clearmont, a station on the C.B. & Q. railroad, was located about twenty-seven miles southeast of Sheridan.

The area is considered a ranching center, but coal has also been found there.

The exact location of **Coalmont** is uncertain. It is known that the coal mining in the area was done by capitalists from Fort Collins, Colorado.

Cokeville still exists northwest of Kemmerer.

The settlement was on the Oregon Short Line railroad.

The town was originally dubbed "Smith's Fork," but the name was changed to Cokeville because of the large deposits of coking coal located nearby. Oddly, some coal was mined in the vicinity, but no coke was ever marketed.[50]

Early newspaper accounts indicate that Joe Fuller was the mortician, and "In his store is a full line of furniture. Everybody looks to him to satisfy their wants along this line."

The population of the town near the turn of the century was about 300, while today it exceeds 400.

Mining in the area was primarily coal-related, but undeveloped gold and silver properties are known to exist as well.

For several years phosphate rock shipments have been made from Cokeville area mines. The phosphate is used in the manufacture of fertilizers.

Part of Cokeville's business district

One of the more imposing structures remaining at Cokeville

The town of **Columbine**, in Natrona County, was probably a Continental Oil Company camp. It was located about four miles south of Midwest.

In its July 9, 1896 issue, the Platte Valley *Lyre* notes that "a reduction plant is being erected at Columbine, this is good business."

Little else is known of this mining town.

Cooper Hill,[51] about thirty-five miles from Laramie, was a copper mining camp for a short time. It is known that postmaster W. C. Fadden had a mine near the town.

Copperopolis grew up on the western end of Casper Mountain. Two men, Bailey and Johnson, found copper in the area and thus gave the town its name.

On March 6, 1891, J. E. Daine and G. E. Butler found gold near the town site, but the gold was not of sufficient quality or quantity to pay mining costs. And so Copperopolis died.

23

Copperton sprang up as a supply point for cattlemen and sheepmen. However, as mining excitement increased in the area, it, like many other towns born and nurtured along the Rudefeha-Encampment tramway, became a mining town.

However, like its sister cities of the Great Encampment, Copperton was doomed to die young.

Its epitaph might read: "R.I.P. Overcapitalized and undermined."

Scattered remains mark the site of this once-bustling copper town.

The Cheyenne *Daily Leader* of July 10, 1895 carried an article mentioning "the newly discovered gold mines at **Cora**," but little else is known of mining in this still-existing town in west-central Wyoming.

The town may have been named for its postmistress, Mrs. Cora Westfall. Other sources believe the settlement was named for a Mrs. Cora M. Beach;[52] but fail to elaborate.

Remains of Copperton are distributed over a fairly large area.

Cumberland is another town that has disappeared. It was located about thirty miles from Kemmerer at the intersection of Muddy Gap and Dry Creek. The town was also situated on a branch line of the Oregon Short Line railroad running from Kemmerer. Like so many Wyoming coal mining settlements, Cumberland was owned by the Union Pacific.

Coal was detected in the area as early as 1840 by explorer John Fremont, but development did not occur until 1900.

At one time Cumberland boasted a population of about 1,800. The local mine produced 2,500 to 3,000 tons of coal daily.[53]

The town had originally been called Camp Muddy, then Reliance, but the coal mines foreman thought Cumberland would be a more appropriate monicker, in remembrance of his Blue Ridge birthplace.

At one time a smallpox epidemic threatened the community. The mine foreman wrote: "We were advised that the only sure cure was good whiskey, applied liberally both internally and externally . . . The pile of whiskey requisitions written looked as though each patient took a daily bath in that delectable fluid, but as we came out without any serious results there were no regrets."[54]

The requisitions for the whisky generally read: "Please deliver to 'hospital' one gallon Old Hickory cured in wood, for bathing Swedes."[55]

The town grew and prospered, then faltered and died in 1930.[56]

Cumberland—*Union Pacific Railroad Museum Collection*

Union Pacific coal mining operations at Cumberland—*Union Pacific Railroad Museum Collection*

Coal camp #7 Cumberland Wyo

One flower offsets the plainness of this marker in the Cumberland cemetery.

One of the more ornate markers in the Cumberland cemetery

An unusual gravesite in the Cumberland cemetery

Typical of the somewhat ornate crosses in the Cumberland cemetery

An unusual marker in the Cumberland cemetery

Cummins City was originally called Jelm.[57] Jelm had been a tie-camp on the Big Laramie River but was converted to a mining town by a number of people who believed John Cummins, his wife, and Doc Thomas—a group that touted some worthless red sandstone as valuable ore.

The history of Jelm stretches back to the 1880s, but it was about 1890 that the unholy trio spread the rumor that the ores in Jelm mountain, in the Copper King lode, needed only capital for development to make investors rich.

Wyoming and eastern capital flowed in. A forty-room, $30,000, three-story hotel was built, along with churches, stamp mills, a jail, and thirty houses. The state's largest waterwheel drove an impressive power plant[58] (although water was in short supply).

Newspaper accounts of 1901[59] tell of a mill being shipped to Jelm from Denver. The item indicates that a new technique was to be used, and that ". . . the amalgamation plates inside the battery [were] so curved that but little splashing [could] occur to lose free gold."

Most men at Jelm worked their claims or were employed by Queen Bee Company at the Copper Queen mine. The company had platted the townsite into 3,000 lots. The Laramie *Boomerang*[60] predicted Jelm would be a city of 1,000 in less than a year and would top 10,000 in less than five years. The paper[61] also stated: "It requires no extraordinary penetration on the part of one experienced in mining matters and conversant with the situation at Jelm today, to see in that camp the making of a great future."

The owners of the Queen Bee and about thirty other properties in the area attempted to attract outside capital. They advertised in a St. Paul, Minnesota, newspaper,[62] "We own forty-two rich claims at and near Jelm, Wyoming, no richer on earth in copper and gold—these properties, worth hundreds of millions, paid for in full, except $15,000 and two years in which to pay for that."

But before long it became clear that the much-touted Copper King lode was valueless. As quickly as they had come, most people left.

The three hoax perpetrators stayed on for several years in the aging hotel, but eventually creditors came after them. Cummins and his wife subsequently headed for Denver, where he died.

A ranch building is all that now occupies the site of Cummins City—a town that many investors would have preferred to forget.

The Union Pacific Coal Company fathered the tent town of **Dana** in 1889. The settlement grew to include sixty-two tenement houses.

One book comments: "Life in Dana was subject to the opulence and fecundity of the high altitude's temperamental wintertimes."[63]

Although it seems an unlikely place for the Union Pacific to bring 200 Blacks to work in the coal mines in January 1900,[64] the company did just that. The experiment failed. According to the same history, "the hot-weather acclimated miners slept in their clothes, and, still shivering from the frostbite of the mountain air, they gave up and went back to their southern sunshine."[65]

While the "Lankies" (miners from Lancashire, England) at Carbon used to enjoy shooting pigeons on the wing, the miners at Dana enjoyed a different sport—betting on the fate of flaming coal cars.

Apparently no system had been designed for catching flying hot coal cinders on the locomotives used to haul coal from the mine area. Frequently, coal in the boxcars would be set afire by flying cinders from the locomotive. Men made wagers on whether the cars would make it to the nearest water tower before the contents went up in flame.

Dana existed for only three years (1889-1891).

Diamondville is one coal mining town whose population has remained fairly stable at 400 since the turn of the century.

In 1868 Harrison Church found a vein of coal about one mile north of where Diamondville was to grow. In the 1870s a company was organized with eastern capital to consolidate extensive mine holdings.

Early in the twentieth century Diamondville's coal output was 3,000 tons per day.[66] The State Board of Immigration, in the early 1900s, was hailing the town as being very modern, sporting a water works facility and electric lights.

Although the veins were not worked until

1894,⁶⁷ they were mined for nearly forty years.

The Diamondville News, founded in February 1898, carried an account of a fire at the No. 1 mine of the Diamond Coal and Coke Company. The fire, of unknown origin, started at 2:30 p.m. December 25, 1898. Jacob Lungreen and several horses were burned to death. The mine was sealed on the day of the fire. It was reopened on January 1, 1899, but because the fire was still burning, the mine was resealed. The record indicates that a fire occurred in the "Diamondville" mine on October 26, 1901, taking twenty-two lives. The "Diamondville No. 1" mine appears again in history on December 2, 1905, when a fire at that location took eighteen lives.⁶⁸

Today Diamondville might be classified as a suburb of Kemmerer, a town that was the scene of two major mine explosions—one in January 1912 which took six lives, and the spectacular explosion of August 14, 1923, which snuffed out ninety-nine lives.

Jakob Turk's "rock grocery" at Diamondville

At least two Wyoming coal mining towns were named **Dietz**, one about four miles north of Sheridan, the other two miles farther north.

Each may have grown to a peak population of 2,500, but probably remained at about 1,000.[69]

The towns were most likely named for C. N. Dietz of Omaha,[70] president of the Sheridan Coal Company, although the Dietz mines were opened in 1893 by C. H. Grinnell,[71] marshall of Sheridan.

A contemporary newspaper account[72] described one Dietz as "a little city of one thousand souls. It has electric lights, water works, churches, schools, secret societies, and other social advantages."

At one time two shaft and three slope mines in the area produced 4,000 tons of coal a day.

Parts of the tipple at Dietz

A part of the tipple at one of the locations of Dietz

The Country Nite Club marks the spot of the location of one of the settlements known as Dietz.

Dillon was founded by former Rudefeha saloon owners who found the location less than one mile from Rudefeha a haven from the antibooze management of the Ferris-Haggarty mine.

Former soldier Malachi[73] W. Dillon opened up a boardinghouse in the new town. According to Pence and Homsher, "... legend runs that he threw his meals in free if customers would patronize his bar."[74] The story continues: "A host of miners found this to their fancy, and logged up their cabin walls nearby. They liked this man called Dillon and said his name would do;"[75] consequently, Dillon was born as a "watering hole" for thirsty miners.

Editor Grant Jones was attracted to Dillon and set up his newspaper the *Doublejack*. The imaginative, heavy-drinking Jones wrote for eastern and midwestern newspapers, providing colorful accounts of the habits of imaginary "coogly woos," "bockaboars," and "one-eyed screaming emus." The coogly woo was a six-legged creature which used a sharp, broad tail to bore holes into which he disappeared. The bockaboar had short legs on the left side and long ones on the right, which made him an admirable mountain climber. The one-eyed screaming emu represented the height of Jones' creativity. The bird ranged on the highest mountain tops and could disappear by swallowing itself.

Jones died in 1903, Dillon in 1915.

For years the attraction at Dillon had been its stilt-supported outhouses—engineered to be accessible above snow level in this high country copper camp.

This structure is Dillon's best

For many years trees have grown inside this log cabin at Dillon

Eadsville was established in 1891 high on Casper mountain, and some rashly predicted it would become an even more important mining camp than Anaconda, Montana.

In January 1891, S. A. (Jack) Currier found "colors" near what was to become Eadsville. But it was probably Charles W. Eads who made the first strike in 1890.[76]

Much money was invested in the gold, silver, lead, galena, asbestos, and copper mines, but little was returned.

It has been estimated that the population of Eadsville grew to almost 5,000[77], but that figure seems too high since only thirteen to fifteen cabins existed in 1891-92.[78]

Eadsville was abandoned five years after it was founded.

The town has become a summer cabin site. Its former character is marked by only a few foundations and the graves of the twin sons of Mr. and Mrs. John Clark. The children died shortly after birth, the first born in Eadsville.

Elwood was a transportation center for the mines in the Sierra Madre mountains, particularly for those near Encampment.

The settlement probably never had more than 100 people, but it was an indispensable transportation point. It was here that freight was loaded onto sleds, which were the only means of transportation appropriate to the usually snow-covered mountainous terrain.

Encampment (Grand Encampment) was originally a trappers' rendezvous. Ranchers settled the area in 1877, and mining began in 1879—the year Ed Haggarty found copper west of Encampment.

The settlement rests at the junction of the North and South forks of the Grand Encampment River.

Possibly in 1901[79] a smelter was erected near the town, and a flume was built to serve the smelter. An estimated 1,200 horsepower of electricity was generated through the system. The town claimed to have the cheapest

View of tramway and Encampment—*Stimson Photo Collection, Wyoming State Archives & Historical Department*

per capita electricity rate of any city in the nation.[80]

The rich ores being mined in the area made it necessary to enlarge the smelter in 1902[81] to a 500-ton capacity. Smelter expansion was undertaken by the North American Copper Company, which also bought the Rudefeha mine in 1903 for one-half million dollars, sold many shares of stock, and built an aerial tramway crossing the Continental Divide. This engineering marvel picked up ore at Rudefeha on the Pacific slope of the Divide, lifted it almost one mile in the air, and dumped it on the Atlantic side at the smelter site near Encampment. Pence and Homsher state that it was the longest aerial tramway in the world—fifteen and three-quarters miles. Another estimate places the tramway length at twenty miles. Perhaps 200,000 tons of ore were carried on it. There is some disagreement about the number of towers that supported the tramway—one estimate is 270,[82] another is 304.[83] It has been estimated that the tramway contained 293,275 feet of steel cable weighing 439,696 pounds.[84] The buckets had a capacity of 900 tons[85] and could deliver 98 tons a day to the furnaces on the river.[86] Reportedly, 1,250,000 feet[87] of timber were used in construction.

In 1906 the concentrating mill at the smelter was destroyed by fire. In 1907 another part of the smelter burned.

The Saratoga and Encampment (Valley) Railroad reached Encampment in 1908, but by that time the smelter was closed and the company was in litigation, accused of overcapitalization and fraud. Useable parts of the smelter were later shipped to South America.[88]

Within three years Encampment's population dwindled to 300.

Today the area is dude ranch country.

Hauling copper from Encampment smelter—
Stimson Photo Collection, Wyoming State Archives & Historical Department

Roasting Ovens, Encampment smelter, Carbon County—*Stimson Photo Collection, Wyoming State Archives & Historical Department*

Concentrating works, Grand Encampment—*Stimson Photo Collection, Wyoming State Archives & Historical Department*

Part of the business district at Encampment

The Encampment opera house has been converted to city offices.

39

Fairbanks (Fairbank) was a copper-smelting town near Guernsey.

The Wyoming Copper Company erected a smelter there in the early 1880s. Coke for the smelter had to be shipped in from Cheyenne, more than 100 miles away. Supplies had to be ferried across the North Platte, increasing transportation costs.

And it turned out that the ores were neither rich nor plentiful, and Fairbanks ceased to exist before the turn of the century.

Ruins of the smelter remain, and the site of Fairbanks is now a park.

Frontier was a coal-mining town in Uinta County on the Oregon Short Line railroad, one and one-fourth miles from Kemmerer.

Large quantities of coal were produced in Frontier.

It was considered a model company town, with electric lights and a water system. The peak population of Frontier was probably about 800.

The mines opened at Frontier in 1900. In 1923 an explosion took the lives of 100 men.

Rescuers recovered the bodies of all but one of the miners. Two days after the explosion, mass funeral services were held at Kemmerer. The Mormon choir from Evanston sang, and several clergymen, including a Greek priest, participated.

One theory purports that the explosion was caused by a miner relighting his lamp.[89]

Gebo may have been named after the Gebo mine, established in 1892 or 1893 by Henry Cottle; or for Sam Gebo, who opened a mine in the area in 1906. For some reason Cottle left Gebo and travelled north to Montana, where he prospected for "Copper King" W. A. Clark.

In 1897-98 Cottle returned to his old find and filed a claim on 160 acres. He was followed by Dad Jones, recently of the Black Hills, who located what later became known as the Crosby mine. Cottle sold part interest in his claim to promoter Sam Gebo and later sold it in its entirety.

Gebo acquired land surrounding the mine with New York money. But President Theodore Roosevelt became suspicious when he learned that $90,000 in fee money had gone to the Lander land office all in one day. The ensuing investigation showed that the money Gebo had raised was used to buy claims under dummy names or under names of dead men. The government cried "fraud," confiscated the land, and kept the $90,000. Gebo escaped justice by fleeing to Guatemala. Through a complex arrangement, the government leased part of the land to the man who had financed the mining land scheme. One writer[90] maintains that this was the first time a mine was leased by the United States government.

In 1906 the railroad had reached Worland, and the mine owners persuaded the railroad to lay a spur to the mine, allowing for considerable expansion. At its peak production the mine employed about 700 men who produced about 100 tons of coal per day.

The Miners' Union put on celebrations at Gebo and nearby **Crosby** on April 1 and Labor Day. All refreshments were free.

A fire destroyed much of the mine, and in twenty-five years the original Cottle, or Gebo, mine had petered out.

Three labor strikes occurred at the mines. During the most far-reaching one, a part of a nationwide strike in 1917, the company called in the militia and hired non-union laborers to man emergency pumps and other equipment. The militiamen searched the houses (there were perhaps 800) looking for whisky and guns. Reportedly they found both.[91]

Nearby was **Kirby**, former shipping point for Gebo coal.

Thomas Sneddon, fresh from Scotland, discovered coal southeast of Diamondville, in the Kemmerer area, and named the resulting town for the city in his native Scotland—**Glencoe**.

Sneddon was tight-fisted, and the most a miner could earn was three dollars for a ten-hour shift.

Many dugouts were built in Glencoe, some of them partially made of shale or wood.

Although it is commonly thought that Cambria was the only place in the West where hard coal was found, one writer[92] maintains that anthracite was also located at Glencoe.

A sort of "suburb" of Glencoe was **Bon Rico**, which contained only two saloons and a dance hall.

Pinched-out coal veins and a mine explosion in which eight[93] men were killed led to the demise of Glencoe in the early 1940s.

Ruins of the town are spread over a large area.

Glenrock (first called Mercedes, then Nuttall, for the man who discovered coal in the area) was one of the few Wyoming coal company towns not owned by the Union Pacific.

The community rests on the bank of the North Platte River twenty-four miles west of Douglas and twenty miles east of Casper.

It is not known how many men the Glenrock Coal Company employed in the mines.

A publication about Wyoming in 1941 says: "Glenrock is an attractive town, with well-built business blocks, modern residences, a refinery, and a sheltered thirty-acre park, on the bank of Deer Creek."[94] The report adds, "The smell of crude oil pervades the place."[95]

Nearby was the site of the Deer Creek Station, established in 1861 as a military post on the Oregon Trail. Indian agent Thomas Twiss lived in the area with his Oglala bride and his pet bear. Major Twiss probably was corrupt, and it was not uncommon to hear the charge that "the major's bear got more sugar than the Indians did."[96]

After removal from office, Twiss and his wife moved to the Powder River to live with her tribe. Only his white beard distinguished him from the Indians, whose ways he adopted.

Glenrock, not a ghost town, has a population of 1,500 today.

A town named **Gold Hill** was spawned near Saratoga (and **La Plata**), but exactly when is not known.

It appears that gold, lead, copper, and silver were found in the region in limited quantities. Ores were crushed in arrastres until 1891, when Colonel Downey installed an eight-stamp quartz mill, concentrator, and cyanide plant.

The camp sported three hotels, three saloons, a blacksmith shop, a school, and a barbershop, run at night by a daytime woodchopper.

According to the Saratoga *Sun*[97], the Saratoga-Gold Hill road left something to be desired, for it was "dangerous to the horses' limbs as well as wearing to a vehicle."

Evidence that nature is gradually reclaiming Gold Hill

Scattered ruins are all that remain of Gold Hill.

The camp of Gold Hill was really a conglomerate of several camps—**Gold City**, **Greenville**, **Golden Courier**, and **Altamont**.[98]

There were two post offices, one at the upper end of the camps, one at the lower.

Little ore was shipped from Gold Hill because miners worked small individual claims. Capital was not attracted to the area to fully develop the ores, since the deposits were not very extensive. However, the Wyoming Consolidated Company was formed by Boston capitalists to mine copper. Frequently shipping costs exceeded ore value.

Still, in the spring of 1894 a Mr. Johnson, dubbed by the Saratoga *Sun*[99] as a "practical miner," was quoted as saying, "You can rest easy about Gold Hill. That camp is coming up and it's going to be the camp of the West. I am willing to stake my reputation as a practical miner on that prediction. There will be more people in Gold Hill inside of four months than ever was there before."

The prediction was erroneous. Today only scattered logs remain to silently speak of Gold Hill's past.

Miners at the Acme mine at Gold Hill—*Western History Research Center, University of Wyoming*

Grass Creek, near the Grass Creek oil fields, still exists, with a population of sixty. In the 1930s the town had 486 residents.

David G. Thomas and a crew of twenty men set out to develop coal deposits at Grass Creek.

The mine was officially closed in 1887, after only seven years of operation.[100]

In 1907 a Mr. Whiting sank an oil discovery well, and the town found temporary renewed life.

Guernsey, with a population of about 800, can hardly be classified as a ghost town. However, it is mentioned because considerable iron and copper from area mines were shipped from this point.

Gunn was apparently established in 1920, or at least that is when it received its first post office. The settlement in Sweetwater County reached a peak population of about 300.

The principal industry was coal mining, under the auspices of the Gunn-Qualy Coal Company.

By 1925 the settlement was no longer listed in the *Wyoming State Business Directory*.

Herman Nickerson and other prospectors founded **Hamilton City**, a camp about four miles east of South Pass City, in 1867 or the following year. A mine just west of town was named **Miner's Delight**, and that was to be Hamilton's new name.

Ore was crushed with an arrastre, and gold was panned from the crushed rock. Later a stamp mill[101] began crushing the ores. At the Miner's Delight mine, $300,000 was recovered during the first few months of operation.[102] Reportedly the Miner's Delight has been dewatered and reworked seven times since 1874.[103]

Miner's Delight was one of the homes of Calamity Jane. She came as a deserted child to Miner's Delight during its first year. Shortly after Calamity had settled in the community, a woman took her to New York to be "properly brought up." As one author put it, "a year later [she] was back, thoroughly educated, and in business for herself."[104] But Calamity Jane did not stay long in Miner's Delight. She moved to Atlantic City, where she operated a dance hall.

One of the better-known miners in the area between 1868 and 1870 was Henry

The sole structure left at Miner's Delight

Comstock, of Comstock Lode fame.[105]

Most writers indicate that Miner's Delight was a boisterous place. But eyewitness James Chisholm wrote: "The miners here are a quiet, industrious class of men, mostly old Californians—very intelligent, and affording more practical information on mining matters than one can derive from mere book students and theorists. There are no idlers in the camp—in fact a professional bummer would very quickly perceive there was no show for him here."[106] However, the same observer did admit that "a vast amount of gold dust is ground in the whisky mill."[107]

The same eyewitness was intrigued by a bear that lived in Miner's Delight. His chronicle of the life and death of the bear reads: "There is a young Grizzly *Bar* in the camp, who is an object of much consideration among the miners. Young 'Cuff' was caught last fall, and has been brought up by hand by John Connor in whose family he resides. He is now a good sized round fat ball of a grizzly, a comical, mischievous kind of a devil, whose bump of acquisitiveness is already strongly developed, and just old enough to be a somewhat dangerous pet, to be handled with care. He has within a week signalized himself by biting a man's arm and tearing a few coatsleeves. Cuffy is after the honey pots all the time. He makes straight for the table when he pays a visit to the neighbors, and if there is no sugar he has very little to say.

"The other day he went up to a cabin when the mother of the family was out, and seeing nothing in the way but the children, he contributed to terrify them by growling like an old bear. The children ran out scared and clammered upon the mud roof, while Cuffy, who had gained his point, went leisurely through the contents of his favorite pots. Once he went into a house, and finding no grub he gave the empty platter such a cuff as sent it ringing to the opposite wall. You cannot hide a pipe from him. He will find it out somehow, and although he is not addicted to the weed it tickles him hugely to handle a pipe. But he is getting altogether too much grizzly, and will have to be converted into dinner by and bye."[108]

Shortly after that entry in his diary, Chisholm reported "My poor friend Cuff is dead. I saw him hanging ignominiously by the hind legs in the meat stall. *Requeiscat in*—that is after I have enjoyed a nice fat tender steak off him."[109]

Chisholm wrote that society in Miner's Delight consisted of three females. One he described as a "plump, dumpling-faced woman built very much in the shape of a bale of cotton drawn together in the middle, and with a big coal scuttle on the top." Of the second woman he wrote: "I don't know who or what she dotes onto." The third, he thought, had a lean, spotty, and unhealthy looking face, and "the upper part of her form is like an old whale bone umbrella not properly folded."[110]

The only two marked graves in the Miner's Delight cemetery

Hanna was first established in 1889 and named for Mark Hanna, influential financier and politician. Hanna claimed that enough coal could be found in the Hanna mines to supply the nation for a century.[111]

Although a school was built during the first year, it was not used because of a lack of pupils.

The Union Pacific Coal Company's No. 1 mine at Hanna was the site of several disasters. On June 30, 1903, an explosion killed 169[112] miners. This left about 150 women widowed and 600 children fatherless. Two explosions in the same mine on March 28, 1908, killed 59 men, leaving 33 widows and 103 fatherless children.[113] The coal company appears to have been profit-hungry and lax in safety precautions. A mine inspector said one of the explosions was caused by the premature opening of an entry into an area in which a fire was burning. According to the district organizer for the United Mine Workers of America, after the 1908 disaster the company gave $800 to each widow and $50 for each surviving child under fifteen.[114]

The Union Pacific shut down its major mines at Hanna in 1954, and Hanna's population dropped from 1,326 to 625 between 1950 and 1960.

In 1970 the population was 460.

No. 1 town, Hanna, founded about 1870 and operative until the 1880s—*Union Pacific Railroad Museum Collection*

No. 2 town, Hanna, founded about 1870 and operative until the 1880s—*Union Pacific Railroad Museum Collection*

No. 3 town, Hanna, founded about 1870 and operative until the 1880s—*Union Pacific Railroad Museum Collection*

A 1924 view of the coaling station at Hanna—*Union Pacific Railroad Museum Collection*

The coaling station at Hanna in 1924—*Union Pacific Railroad Museum Collection*

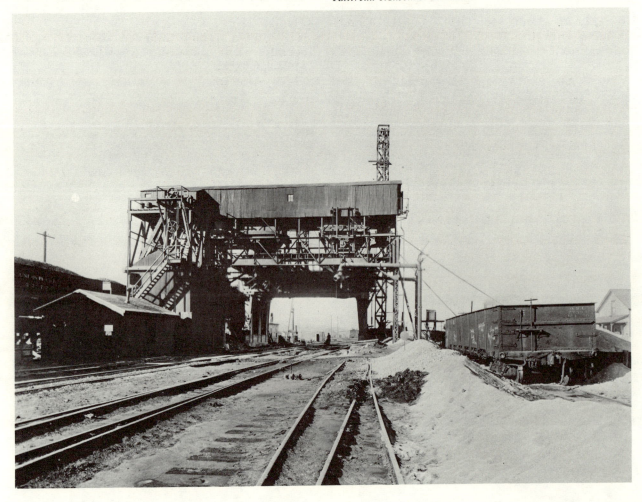

Any bets on which will first succumb to Mother Nature at Hanna?

One of many abandoned structures at Hanna

Hartville grew up north of Guernsey on the Colorado and Northwestern Railroad line. It traces its beginnings to a copper strike in the region in 1881. More than one million tons of ore were shipped from the Hartville and Sunrise mines.

Most of the miners were of Italian and Greek backgrounds, and operas performed at Hartville were usually sung in those languages.

Coal and iron mines were also in operation near Hartville.

There is some dispute as to how Hartville got its name. One version is that it was named for Colonel Verling K. Hart, who is sometimes credited with fathering the town. The other version explains that the town was named for its first mayor, James Hart.[115]

The town had many characters, among whom were Snake River Jack, Montana Bill, The Oglala Kid, Red, Blackie, The White Swede, Cotton, Three-fingered Charlie, Step-and-a-half John, Sister Mary, Vinegar Bill, Rattlesnake Dick, Calico Jack, Jerky Bill, and Woodbox Jim.[116]

The town boasted concrete sidewalks near the turn of the century—an uncommon convenience in early Wyoming.

The village still exists.

The main street of Hartville

The Hartville town hall

The Hartville fire department

Hecla was established on Middle Crow Creek. Its mines have been worked intermittently since the late 1880s.

Prospectors came to the area in search of gold, silver, and copper.

Ruins of a brick kiln, a copper smelter, log cabins, and adobe houses are scattered among ranch buildings and corrals.

Iron Mountain was named for the large iron deposits that were mined about six miles from the settlement.

Iron Mountain, now a ghost town, is where western badman Tom Horn is thought to have mistakenly killed a ten-year-old[117] boy named Willie Nickell. Horn was subsequently hanged.

Johnstown was one of the shortest-lived mining towns in Wyoming.

In 1892 a group of men from Chicago organized the Syndicate Improvement Company, capitalized at $3 million.

Machinery was installed, men were hired, and Johnstown was built. However, within two years the project collapsed.

Keystone still exists south of Centennial.

The town had an "up again-down again" mining history. The Lode Mining Company built a mill at Keystone, probably in 1872; it later closed. Evidence indicates that the mill was run for two days in 1938. It was dismantled in the summer of 1955.[118]

Today Keystone is a sleepy little mountain village.

Kirwin was located about thirty-five miles up Wood River, southwest of Meeteetse.

The town apparently existed in 1906 and 1907, with a peak population of 300.

Contemporary newspaper accounts indicate that mining exploration occurred in the area as late as 1969.[119] At that time access to the town site was blocked by the company doing the exploration work, but reportedly several old structures and an assay office remain.

Lamont was an oil town north of Rawlins. It was named for a homesteader named Jimmie Lamont, who had a small store in his home.

Oil activity increased in the area, a post office was established in Lamont's store, and the settlement was officially named.

Lysite, southeast of Thermopolis, was named in memory of Jim Lysite (or Lysaght), a miner and prospector who was killed by Indians in the early 1870s near Lysite Mountain.

Probably one of the few remaining original structures at Keystone

It is not known how many different locations **Lavoye** occupied, but there were several. This "now-here-now-there" oil town was named for its founder, Louis Lavoye, and was a product of the Salt Creek oil fields.

Over 1,000 people lived in Lavoye when an oil corporation holding mineral rights to the land under the town decided to claim surface rights as well.

The corporation accused the citizens of being "squatters" on company land. The people refused to move, but found company legal pressures and pressures from the ends of high-pressure hoses persuasive. The hoses sprayed them with oil.

After three years of litigation, the company won, and in 1925 the United States Department of the Interior decided that people must move on to make room for the company oil wells.

Lavoye was moved so many times that an anonymous poet paraphrased an old lyric to "where is my wandering Lavoye tonight?"

Only a few barely discernible foundations mark the remains of one quasi-permanent location of Lavoye—a wandering Wyoming oil town.

Lavoye—*Western History Research Center, University of Wyoming*

The Platte Valley *Lyre* of July 9, 1896, noted in passing that a labor strike occurred in the mines at **Leadville**. It was also mentioned that Leadville was a ten-hour camp—meaning the miners pulled ten-hour, rather than eight-hour, shifts.

The settlement seems to have completely disappeared.

The lost camp of **Leslie** prospered briefly because of copper and iron.

Where it was founded, when it died are not known.

Lewiston was founded in 1879, consisting of twenty-five buildings that included four saloons.

The town grew up around the Burr (first called the Strawberry) vein in the Antelope Hills. One unusual aspect of Lewiston was that several mines were located within the city limits.

Vacant houses from Camp Stambaugh were moved to Lewiston, and in 1882 a general store was built.

Much "salted" mining property changed hands in Lewiston: as one writer[120] put it, "Each 'sucker' salted in turn, and made money selling to the next buyer."

A store and a livery stable are the only structures that remain in Lewiston. Nearby are the water-filled mines.

Lewiston

The largest still-standing structures at Lewiston

Many bullets went through this door on the large structure left at Lewiston.

This crude marker is along the Oregon Trail at Lewiston.

Manville still exists about twenty-eight miles west of the Nebraska line and eight miles from Lusk.

Farming and the cattle industry thrive here, but the settlement also saw mining activity. In the 1920s more than 100 oil rigs operated in the immediate vicinity.

Something got lost in the translation when **McFadden** was named for early-day Ohio Oil production man John McFayden.

McFayden had been an oil hauler, a pumper, a roustabout, a blacksmith, a carpenter, and a tool dresser. Like many others, he was without money or work during the depression of 1893. Somehow he made it through those dark days and later worked at making barrels. Still later, McFayden leased some land, rented an oil-drilling rig, and drilled a well. It was a dry hole.

In 1894 he was hired by Ohio Oil Company to fight brush fires. This proved to be a good move for McFayden, who ultimately became vice president of Ohio Oil and director of production for the company in California.

McFadden still exists northwest of Laramie.

Midwest, a still-surviving town, grew up near the Teapot Dome United States Naval Oil Reserve in east-central Wyoming. It was described in the 1920s as a typical oil company town.

One man wrote, "I was informed that every male adult in the place was an employee, or connected with the Pacific Refining Company in some capacity and they, with their families, constitute the entire population of the camp."[121]

The town was named "Midwest" because the early settlers thought it to be the middle of the West.[122]

Midwest was initially called "Home Camp" because it formed the nucleus of other outlying camps. Nearby was **Peckville**, named for Reverend Oscar Peckenpaugh, in whose house the post office was established.

A fire in 1948 burned down the Midwest grocery store and shopping center. The town also had a hospital which was abandoned in 1936.

Millersburg was a community of miners and prospectors on the North Platte River, where the town of Guernsey now stands.

Cheyenne cattleman Colonel A. T. Babbitt and Chicago capitalists organized the Wyoming Copper Company, which bought the Sunrise mine and built a smelter on the North Platte one mile above Millersburg.

Mineral Hill is a relatively new ghost town, having been founded in the early 1930s.

The fairly large Mineral Hill mill still stands and occasionally is operated.

Most of the remains of Mineral Hill (several mine structures and one dozen cabins) are strung along Spotted Tail Creek. One of the reasons for the settlement's relatively well-preserved condition is that the owners do not welcome visitors.

Mineral Hill—*Wyoming Travel Commission*

A remnant of the past, this crumbling stamp mill is testimony to the mining activity carried on in the Black Hills region of Wyoming at the ghost town of Mineral Hill near the Wyoming-South Dakota border. Mineral Hill is a modern day ghost town, having enjoyed its finest hour in the 1930s. Nearby Welcome, Wyoming, was a turn-of-the-century mining town predecessor, and several crumbling buildings, foundations, and rusting pieces of mining equipment can still be seen at both mining camps—*Wyoming Travel Commission*

One-half mile from Mineral Hill is the site of **Welcome**, a gold camp where a twenty-stamp mill was built. Still standing—among a few other tattered remains—is a pump house, probably used to pump water to the mills at Tinton, South Dakota.

Welcome—*Wyoming Travel Commission*

Monarch, ten miles northwest of Sheridan, began as a coal town on the Chicago, Burlington, and Quincy railroad in October 1903.[123]

Peak production was about 2,000 tons of coal daily. Maximum population probably did not exceed about 800.[124]

Most of the town was razed several years ago by a construction firm involved in strip coal mining in Montana and Wyoming. As of this writing, only a few structures remain.

The October 22, 1903 edition of the Sheridan *Post* reported that Stewart Kennedy and friends were building a mining camp at their new mine and that the camp was named Monarch. At that time the company was building thirty-six dwellings, a store, blacksmith and carpenter shops, and a schoolhouse. At its zenith, there were 169 dwellings in Monarch.

Only union miners worked the Monarch mine—three shifts of eight hours each.

The company store at Monarch

The stone church at Monarch

There are few unbroken windows at the company structures at Monarch.

A study in contrasts at the Monarch cemetery

The Evangelical Lutheran cemetery at Monarch as sundown approaches

This marker, featuring a lamb, indicates where Julia Sturtz is buried in the Monarch cemetery. She died before she was two years old.

Oakley was located two and one-half miles south of Kemmerer and was considered to be a suburb of Diamondville (Diamondville, in turn, is considered to be a suburb of Kemmerer). Perhaps up to 300 Oakley residents were employed by the Diamond Coal and Coke Company.

The population in 1921 was listed as twenty-five. Shortly thereafter the settlement disappeared.

Parco exists, but not in name.

In 1922-23 the Producers and Refiners Corporation built a refinery and model town for 1,500 persons six miles east of Rawlins. The "Wonder Town of Wyoming" with its unusual Spanish architecture was named "Parco" for the initials of the company.

The Sinclair Oil Company acquired the property in 1934 and changed the name to **Sinclair**.

The Union Pacific depot at Parco (Sinclair) as it appeared in 1925—*Union Pacific Railroad Museum Collection*

Piedmont's history popularly revolves around an incident involving Thomas C. Durant, vice president and chief promoter of the Union Pacific railroad.

Durant had been persistently[125] pushing the thin steel ribbons of the Union Pacific across Wyoming, intent on joining Central Pacific[126] rails at Promontory, Utah. But Durant had neglected to pay his Irish raillayers. The workmen surrounded Durant's railroad car in Weber Canyon, near Piedmont, and refused to let the man or the elegant gilt work, inlaid woodwork-bedecked, crystal-chandeliered, mirror-lined private car move until he had paid them five months of back pay. Durant wired for $500,000 and paid the men, but that incident, plus rain-caused delays, postponed the golden spike-driving festivity at Promontory Summit for two days, from May 8 until May 10, 1869.

A directors' meeting of the Union Pacific held in Thomas C. Durant's private car. Durant is seated second from right. On his left is John Duff; on his right is Sidney Dillon. Next to Dillon is Silas Seymour—*Union Pacific Railroad Museum Collection*

Dr. Durant and party at Green River—*Union Pacific Railroad Museum Collection*

Thomas C. Durant, Union Pacific vice president and chief promoter—*Union Pacific Railroad Museum Collection*

Parts of the sombre remains of Piedmont

The "beehive" charcoal kilns at Piedmont were built in 1869 by Moses Byrne to supply the Pioneer smelter in the Utah Valley.

Platinum City was established in the late 1920s by prospectors searching in the Centennial Mountain mining district for the lost Downey lode. They found traces of platinum, along with gold, silver, and copper.

Promoters brought in mining equipment and platted a city, complete with powerhouse.

The mine, however, did not meet operating expenses, and in 1938 the government confiscated the property.

The land, the mining machinery, household articles, and everything else in town, valued at more than $100,000, were sold at public auction for $7,000.

What little remains of Platinum City (parts of a power generating plant and refinery) is in a privately owned hay meadow.[127]

Little is known of **Ragtown**—one of Wyoming's earliest mining camps.

In about 1880 British sportsman-author William A. Baillie-Grohman[128] wrote that the settlement consisted of "a few burnt logs, and a rusty gun-barrel or two," and that this was "all that remains of Ragtown, which is said to have been the most elevated mining camp of the day."

Baillie-Grohman also reported that about twenty Ragtowners had been the victims of "redskins' scalping knives." Said he, "[their] unwise intrepidity resulted in the loss of their hair—and lives."[129]

It was at Ragtown that Ed Haggarty (discoverer of the Ferris-Haggarty mine at Rudefeha) saw Mike Whalen try to get an early start on the mining season. Whalen piled his equipment and supplies on a large sled, to which he attached a long rope. Fellow miners were to then lower him and the sled onto a long, snow-covered slope that led to his mining claims. Whalen crawled on top of the sled, and his friends began to lower him. Half-way down the slope the rope broke, and sled and miner dropped into a snowbank. But, as Haggarty described it, the fall only "broke two eggs and Mike's feelings." However, Haggarty indicated, "Mike was melting the snow around him with a volume of names directed at his helpers."[130]

Early day Rambler—*Western History Research Center, University of Wyoming*

Rambler was born to satisfy the needs of miners from the Doane-Rambler and other mines in the area.

The Doane-Rambler was discovered in 1879. The copper from the mine was spectacularly rich. Reportedly, several carloads of copper from the mine averaged 51 percent pure metal.

Rambler consisted of two hotels, three grocery stores, two saloons, and several other businesses.

A marker near Rambler indicates where Thomas Alva Edison supposedly conceived the idea for the incandescent lamp. It has been said that Edison caught his bamboo fishing pole in a tree, and in an attempt to free the pole he tried to break it. Being unsuccessful, he lit a match to the pole and noted how white and long it burned, still retaining its shape. This principle he applied to the electric light bulb.

In recent years a sheep company used the cadaverous structures at Rambler as headquarters. But today only one log cabin remains.

The Thomas A. Edison monument near Rambler

A diminuative cabin is all that remains of Rambler.

A camp called **Red Canyon** was the site of a mine explosion that killed sixty-one men in March 1895. The camp was located about seven miles south of Lander.

Richieville was located at an undetermined date about forty-five miles from Laramie and nine miles south of the Rambler mine on Lake Creek. This location was in the center of a diversified mining belt. The settlement consisted of about one dozen log houses and as many tents. The Laramie Boomerang[136] reported "A park opening at the front of the houses and the trees at the back combine scenery and economy of domestic materials seldom united."

In the same edition, the "social life" of Richieville was described: "The social life of Richieville is something inspiring to the city guest. Huge bonfires every evening lighting up the surrounding crags and peaks and the dark shadows of the trees serve to enhance the art of the musicians and story tellers who are ever ready to respond to the call for entertainment as the whole camp gathers, as did a patriarchal family, around the hearthstone of yore."[137]

Riverside was located one mile north of Encampment.

Before it became a mining camp, Riverside had served as a bartering site for Whites and Indians.

Later, a wayside station was set up by a man named Doggett—for whom the settlement was first named. However, when mining activities began the name was changed to Riverside.

By 1901 the town had sixty buildings,[131] including a forty-room hotel and two saloons.

Unlike most mining towns, Riverside did not die, and today a few people still live there. As Pence and Homsher put it, "Like grandma in the old rocking chair, Riverside on the Encampment is handing down to its grandchildren, to those little boys with willow fishing poles and to those little girls in bright blue jeans, a memory recalling Old Wyoming's bygone days."[132]

A typical Riverside residence

The old and new intermingle at Riverside.

71

Remains of foundations of the Riverside smelter

Rock Springs is hardly a ghost town, but because it is a former mining town, it is included in this volume.

The town was first settled in 1875, representing the first great coal strike in Wyoming.

The Clark Hose Company, a group of twenty-four volunteer firemen, was organized at Rock Springs early in 1891. The firemen initially rode horses to fires but later switched to bicycles.

Chinese were imported to work the Union Pacific Coal Company mines, and by 1885 about 1,000 Chinese resided at Rock Springs. White workers, believing that the company favored the Chinese and discriminated against the natives, mobbed Chinatown on September 2, 1885, burning it and killing about thirty Chinese.[133] The rioting spread to other towns. The frightened Chinese walked the railroad tracks and were picked up by the railroad (whose subsidiary had hired them) and given a modicum of protection. Later, the United States government paid $147,000[134] for their losses (Wyoming could not pay; it was not yet a state).

The Wyoming General Hospital, a miners' hospital created by legislative act, was opened at Rock Springs in 1894. The facility was established to give medical care and surgical attention to disabled miners.

The major Rock Springs mines were shut down in 1954; however, today Rock Springs is a thriving town of about 12,000, comprising an estimated forty-one nationalities.[135]

The Rock Springs depot in the early 1880s—*Frank Harmer Collection*

In 1897 Ed Haggarty, grubstaked by James Rumsey, Robert Deal, and George Ferris, found copper. They staked twenty acres and created a name for the area from the first two letters of each last name—Ru-de-fe-ha. The next year Deal and Rumsey backed out, leaving only Ferris and Haggarty to develop the mine, which they renamed the Ferris-Haggarty. In either 1897[138] or 1899[139] Haggarty sold his interest in the Ferris-Haggarty; in 1900 Ferris died in an accident caused by a spooked horse.

The town that grew up in the area of the mine was called **Rudefeha**.

However, as it is written, "Slowly, but surely, mismanagement, over-capitalization resulting in costly litigation, hazardous transportation, and the Rockies' determination to keep their minerals, pronounced the death sentence of the mine."[140]

Savery is a small town south of Rawlins which had little, if anything, to do with mining. Nevertheless, it was named for an early day prospector and trapper.

Rudefeha—*Western History Research Center, University of Wyoming*

Compressed air locomotive in Ferris-Haggerty mine—*Stimson Photo Collection, Wyoming State Archives & Historical Department*

More Sheridan Area Ghost Towns

Acme still exists, and coal is being strip mined by the Big Horn Coal Company. During its heyday the population was 800; today it is 125.

The horse barn at Acme

The post office and general store at Acme

Carneyville (Carney) was a coal-mining town founded in 1904 about nine miles northwest of Sheridan.

The settlement was fathered by Roy Carney and named for either him or his brothers. Later, the town was renamed Kleenburn, the trade name of the coal mined in the area.

The town was served by the Chicago, Burlington, and Quincy railroad.

The cemetery and several structures remain.

Little is known about **Hotchkiss**, which presumably had at one time a population of several hundred.[141]

Kleenburn (Carneyville) was squeezed between Acme and Monarch. It reached a peak population of about 1,000. Approximately 4,000 tons of coal a day were taken from the Carney Coal Company's coal mines.

The saloon in Kleenburn proclaimed that it featured Sheridan Export Beer.

The Interstate highway cuts near the edge of the cemetery in the Kleenburn-Monarch-Acme area.

Kooi (pronounced "coy"), also north of Sheridan, was named for Peter Kooi, who came to Wyoming from Chicago in 1904. Kooi assisted in opening and developing mining operations of the Wyoming Coal Mining Company at Monarch. In April 1907 he opened his own mine at Kooi.

Unlike the buildings in many company towns, houses at Kooi were painted different colors.

Fourth of July celebrations at Kooi featured free pop, sandwiches, and beer. The celebrations began when the camp band marched to the bandstand for the traditional flag raising. The day ended with a fireworks display and the lighting of oil barrel fires on the hillsides. Probably no more than 400 men were employed in the mine, and the weekly payroll reached about $50,000.

The town had a general store, a post office, a pool hall, a schoolhouse, a church, a community hall where films were shown, and a town baseball team.

There were about 250 homes, a boardinghouse, and bachelor quarters at Kooi.

In 1920 Kooi was sold to Peabody Coal Company.[142] Now the town is gone.

Kuzaraville, established a couple of miles north of Sheridan, consisted of a mine, a store, and a few houses. It had no post office.[143]

Model was a coal-mining camp located near Sheridan. It was established in 1911.

Silver Cliff (also called **New Rochelle, Running Water,** and **Lusk**) was born in 1879 when the Great Wyoming (or Western) Mining and Milling Company began mining the first silver deposits in Wyoming. A large crusher was built at Silver Cliff in 1884. The operations were near what is referred to as "Mining Hill." Limited amounts of gold and copper were also found at Mining Hill, but they did not account for much of the overall production.

Because of the nature of the silver-bearing quartz, mining in the Silver Cliff area was difficult and expensive. About $32,000 was spent on the operation, and then the project was dropped. To date, silver has not been profitably mined in Wyoming.[144]

Silver Cliff was a rough town, perhaps in part because it was on the Cheyenne-Deadwood stage route.

One of the town's characters was Old Mother Feather Legs,[145] who ran a whorehouse in a dugout. In the "fun house" cellar Old Mother Feather Legs hid her money and her booze. Dangerous Dick Davis sold "tangle-leg,"[146] which she distilled, probably for more than it was worth. Rumor had it that the unsavory pair had a liaison with road agents.

Old Mother Feather Legs was found dead in 1879, bullet holes in her back. Dangerous Dick vamoosed with an estimated $1,500 in cash.

No one knew Old Mother Feather Legs' real name; but it "came to light" years later when Dangerous Dick was apprehended by the law. Just prior to his hanging, he confessed that he was an outlaw known as "The Terrapin," and that Old Mother Feather Legs was Mam Shepard, mother of desperadoes Tom and Bill Shepard.

All that remains of Silver Cliff is a large barn which had been situated along the Deadwood-Cheyenne stage line.

Silver Crown (or Silver City) was established near the Fort Russell Military Reservation in 1885. At Silver Crown was located the Carbonate Belle, a mine salted by Professor Aughey. Some were duped into thinking that the Carbonate Belle was the greatest bonanza since the Comstock Lode. Cheyenne businessmen said they would put one-half million dollars into development. But Wilbur C. Knight, a geology professor at the University of Wyoming, exposed the hoax, and the development was stopped.

The last time Silver Crown made the news was October 7, 1935, when a transport plane crashed there, killing twelve persons.

Many historic events predated the founding of **South Pass City**. Among them, in 1842 a trapper from Georgia found gold nuggets in the high tributaries of the Sweetwater River. He tied the nuggets in his tobacco sack; they were found with his body.

In 1855 a party of gold seekers returning from the California fields found rich traces of gold. However, blizzards forced them to retreat to warmer climes for the winter, with the intention of returning. The next spring, two days out from Fort Laramie, the prospectors were overtaken by troops who escorted them back to the fort for unknown reasons. The group disbanded.

Three years later the leader of the former group prospected the area along the Sweetwater. In 1860 he and eight others found gold and began mining in Strawberry Gulch.

In 1861 mountain man H. G. Nickerson mined in the gulch where the rich Carissa lode was to be discovered years later.

During the summer of 1864, Lieutenant William Brown and his company of soldiers did some prospecting along the Sweetwater. They found one lead north of Rock Creek and named it the Buckeye.[147]

In either 1865[148] or 1866[149] Tom Ryan, a member of a detachment of troops,[150] found gold in the same area. The discovery was to become known as the Carissa lode.[151] Later, others located the outcroppings which brought on a gold rush to the Carissa lode in 1867.

Ryan, after being mustered out of the military, returned to the area, only to find his claim jumped. But he kept his cool and found another lode—the Carter (later renamed the Robert Emmett).

By October 1867 South Pass City was laid out, and by the end of the following year the town had a population variously estimated at from 2,000[152] to 4,000.[153] By the end of 1869 South Pass City had become the seat of government in Sweetwater County and by

79

1872 had become the largest[154] city in the territory.

The prospectors were trespassing on Indian hunting grounds. In retaliation, the Sioux, Arapahoes, and Cheyennes stole horses, mules, goods, and money, and took lives. During Indian raids women and children were locked in a cavelike recess behind a merchant's wine cellar.

Scalped and mutilated miners' bodies were left as examples of what might happen to other Whites. The Indians faced and overcame a problem when it came to scalping Bill Rose, a somewhat bald South Passer. For their trophy the Indians cut off his side hair and one ear. Additionally, they cut out the sinews of his arms for tying steel heads to their arrows and sinews from his back for bowstrings. As one observer put it, "poor Bill seems to have been pretty much used up."[155]

James Chisholm, a Scotsman who wrote for the Chicago *Times*, thought the booze in South Pass City was "poison" and set out to prove the point. "To show the quality of the poison they keep here," he wrote, "I may mention that a few tastes brought me to my level and today I am more dead than alive—can't get around at all—can't write—can't eat—can't think."[156]

South Pass City became something of a mecca for music lovers. The city opera house was called the Overland Exchange Hall, and here the Carter Troupe played *Lucretia Borgia* in 1868[157] or 1869.[158]

Yet, the settlement lacked some necessities, as evidenced by a letter from South Pass City dated March 7, 1867. It said: "One [problem] is the total lack of gum boots, without which it is almost impossible to do any work, and another is the weather will hardly admit of it."[159]

Chisholm, in his *Journal of the Wyoming Gold Rush*, described an 1868 view of South Pass City by boasting that "disreputable" persons were not present; that " . . . at present we are far removed from them. Compared with that we are living in a kind of Arcadia—an Arcadia with a little whisky now and then to sweeten it."[160]

In 1869, when Wyoming came into full territorial status, Mrs. Esther Morris of South Pass City supposedly held a tea party for about forty persons in her home. Some say[161] that among those in attendance were the two

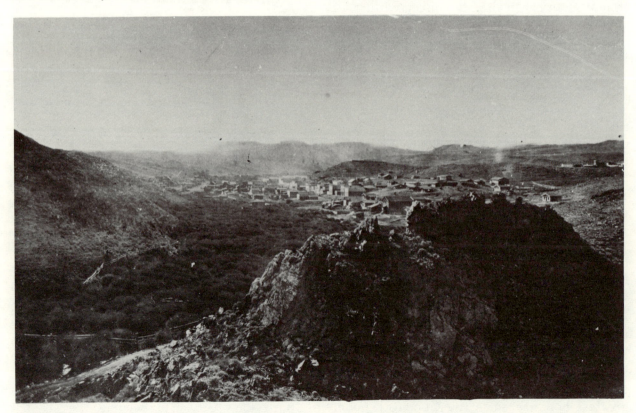

South Pass City—*Western History Research Center, University of Wyoming*

candidates for the Territorial Legislature—W. H. Bright and Captain H. Nickerson. Mrs. Morris extracted a promise from both men that whoever won the election would introduce a measure granting women the right to vote, hold public office, and receive compensation equal to that given men. Current knowledge indicates that Mrs. Morris did not meet Colonel Bright until some time after the tea party.162 The measure became law when Governor John Campbell signed it; it was the first women's suffrage law in the nation.

In 1870 Mrs. Morris was appointed Justice of the Peace (another first). None of her decisions163 were ever overruled by a higher court, suggesting that she did a good job.

As the ores became more difficult and expensive to mine, South Pass City began to die. By 1878 the town was almost completely deserted. An eyewitness to the death throes put it this way: "Well, the excitement has all died away and Sweetwater has been voted by the unanimous voice of hundreds of disappointed bummers—a humbug. Still yonder it lies, waiting a proper inspection, waiting for capital and human energy to develop its resources. Sweetwater was not so much the humbug, however, as the inexperienced incapables who went there, with no money and no knowledge, the crowds of busted individuals who thought gold could be gathered like pebbles, the traders who brought goods to a market where nothing was to be had in exchange—they were the humbugs. That was the trouble. I am told that numbers came there who simply lay around the camp for a week drinking whisky and were too indolent even to look at the ledges—then departed, preaching humbug."164

South Pass—*Stimson Photo Collection, Wyoming State Archives & Historical Department*

The report continued: "Between South Pass City at 3 o'clock in the morning and South Pass at 3 o'clock in the afternoon there is but little difference. The actual residents number not over 50 or 60.[165] There are some 50 dwellings but the greater part of them are either forsaken, or were never inhabited . . . I see a number of stores in the main street, with attractive fronts all brand new—not one of which seems to have been occupied."[166]

In 1885 South Pass briefly revived when development work was done in the Carissa mine. Another flurry of activity came in 1933 when dredges were used in the old placer ground.

Today South Pass City is one of Wyoming's best-preserved ghost towns. Preservation efforts have been made, and as a consequence it is listed in the National Register of Historic Places.

Part of South Pass' main street

South Pass City—*Wyoming Travel Commission*

South Pass

The dance hall at South Pass

An impressive mill near South Pass City

Slack, Wyoming

Slack was located on Pass Creek west of Parkman.

The settlement was on the Bozeman Trail, hacked out by a group of men led by John Bozeman. The trail, started in 1866, went from Fort Laramie, Dakota Territory, to Bozeman, Montana Territory.

During its heyday Slack had a post office, a church, some stores, and houses.

Today, the remnants of Slack can be found on the Woodson Moss Ranch.

Spring Valley was established in 1899 when the Union Pacific opened mines in the vicinity. However, coal had been discovered in the region in 1868 either by soldiers who were patrolling the area or by Russell Thorp, Sr., one-time owner of the Cheyenne and Black Hills Stage Company.[167] Many houses from Almy were moved to Spring Valley, and some brick structures were built to house the 300 families who were moved to the company town.

Unfortunately, wells drilled for water yielded oil, and water had to be supplied to residents by railroad tank cars. Oil seeped into the coal mines, creating real and potential gas explosion problems.

As a result, the Spring Valley mines were sealed in 1905.

Mining equipment and most homes were moved to Hanna after the mine closings.

Sublett (Sublet or Sublette) was a coal-mining town apparently housing employees of the Kemmerer Coal Company. Its peak population was perhaps 350. Sublett was abandoned in 1934, and the *Wyoming Historical Blue Book* reports a 1940 population of zero.

The dry, but poignant, U.S. Bureau of Mines report of a mine explosion at the No. 5 Sublet[t] mine on September 16, 1924, which killed thirty-nine men, reads:

> The explosion about 11:45 a.m., gave little surface evidence; two distinct reports and a cloud of dust came from the mouth of the rock slope. Most of the 39 victims were quickly killed by flame and suffocation. Twelve men of the 7 south entry walked out of the rock slope some hours after the explosion. Rescue experts and crews with apparatus were gathered from neighboring mines and from a distance, and labored until Oct. 14 to restore ventilation and recover the bodies, under the difficulties of rock falls, flooded workings, and general wreckage. The 12 north entry in which the explosion originated was caved for almost the entire length. Enough gas was regularly given off in the mine to entail immediate hazard if ventilation was even temporarily interrupted. Edison electric cap lamps were used; but regular tests for gas were neglected. Dust was sprinkled on entries and slope. Gas accumulated in 12 north when a timber crew deranged a line curtain; it was ignited by an arc from a locomotive trolley. Dust and gas spread the explosion to almost all parts of the mine. Rock dusting, improved ventilation, and permissible equipment were recommended.[168]

Sunrise was fathered by the Colorado Fuel and Iron Company.

At one time the town was the terminus of the Colorado and Wyoming railroad and had a population of 1,000.

The town was established in 1903[169] after eastern capital began developing the iron ore deposits in the area.

It has been said that one of the camp founders—George Eaton—was so impressed with a sunrise that he so named his claim, and the town was also named accordingly.

John Landon, George Eaton, and Jeff McDonald located the first copper claim in 1881.[170]

The W.P.A. files at the Wyoming State History Department indicate that in 1901 no houses existed in Sunrise and that miners' families stayed in neighboring Hartville.

Sunrise is the site of the huge iron ore pit known as the Glory Hole, or Chicago mine. At one time it was the largest iron mine west of the Mississippi River.[171]

Some of the 104 company-built garages at Sunrise

Miners at the Sunrise mines, Sunrise, Wyoming—
Wyoming State Archives and Historical Department

General offices of the Sunrise mine at Sunrise

A total of six mines were operated in **Superior** (known as Reliance until July 14, 1906). The last to be put in operation—the D.O. Clark, constructed in 1938—was expected to have sufficient coal to operate for three-quarters of a century.

Superior still exists, northeast of Rock Springs, shrunken in population from 1,150 in 1940 to a handful today.

Pacific Power and Light Company facilities at Reliance

One of several large structures remaining at Reliance

The Reliance mill

Portrait of a dead company town:
Superior, Wyoming

92

93

It appears that a coal mining town called **Sweetwater** was located about five miles southwest of Rock Springs. At its peak, Sweetwater may have had a population of 300.

Tie Siding was generally thought to be a railroad town because it supplied timber for the Union Pacific.

At one time it was estimated that 1,000 choppers worked in the woods in the Tie Siding area.

The town was established in 1868. However, as the need for timber dwindled, so did Tie Siding, and in 1931 the post office was moved one mile west of the old site.

Sometime during the town's earlier history, copper ores were found in the vicinity, but it is not clear if any were successfully mined.

View of Tie Siding—*Stimson Photo Collection, Wyoming State Archives & Historical Department*

A camp north of Evanston named **Twin Creeks** was operated from 1881 to 1885 by the Union Pacific.

Twin Creeks coal was used as fuel for the Oregon Short Line Railroad.

Two mines were opened, but the lignite mined was of inferior quality; consequently, the mines were closed in 1885, four years after the Union Pacific Coal Department first bought them.

During peak production, 400 men worked in the mines. Twin Creek's population probably reached 1,500.[172]

When the mines closed, Twin Creek structures were moved to nearby Rock Springs.

By most definitions **Upton**, with a population of about 1,000, is not a ghost town, but part of its history is related to mining.

Upton was first named Irontown because of the iron deposits in the area. When it shifted from mining town to sheep town, the name was appropriately changed to Merino, for a breed of sheep. Then, when the settlement was evolving into a transportation center, the townspeople decided to change the name again. Some wanted "Neeley," but those who preferred "Upton" won. Some say that the settlement was named for John Upton, a member of the Stuart Mining Expedition of 1864; others maintain that it was named for a livestock agent named Upton.

Bentonite mining is currently carried on in the area.

Walcott was a transportation center for nearby mines.

One writer maintains that between 1890 and 1910 Walcott was the busiest railroad loading point between Omaha, Nebraska, and Ogden, Utah.[173] At Walcott mining machinery was hauled in and copper ore shipped out.

Some gold, coal, and silver mining occurred in the Walcott area. One tale relates that coal miner W. W. Petty noticed a silver coating on the grate of his stove in which he was burning Rock Cliff Coal Company coal. This led to a short-lived spurt in silver mining, financed through the locally supported Rock Cliff Coal Company.

The town consisted of a hotel, a depot, two livery stables, several stores and saloons, and a population of several hundred.

However, when the boom at Encampment turned to a bust, the highway bypassed the town, the Union Pacific depot was removed in 1940, and Walcott expired.

A "new" Walcott grew up along the highway.

The picturesque "Glub Saloon" and a few other structures remain of "old" Walcott.

Winton was located fourteen miles north of Rock Springs. Originally it was called Megeath, for G. W. Megeath, organizer and promoter of the coal company camp (the name was changed in 1921).

The coal town was established to meet coal supply needs created by World War I. During its peak, 300 to 400 miners were employed in the Union Pacific mines.

Afterword

Other ghost towns can be found in Big Wyoming, but few had anything to do with mining.

The compendium would include, but not be limited to, Holmes, Stringtown, Rock Creek, Percy, Brownsville, Benton, Old Town (Green River), Bryan, Spring Valley, Bothwell, Bessemer, Antelope, Jireh, Donkeytown, Suggs, Woodrock, Marquetta, Andersonville, Old Town (Thermopolis), Hazard, Woods Landing, Wyoming, Lookout, Wilcox, Como, Victoria, Miser, Sampo, St. Mary's, Swan, Separation, Filmore, Creston, Latham, Washakie, Red Desert, Table Rock, Black Butte, Salt Wells, Wilkins, Marston, Moxa, Nutria, Twin Creek, Church Butte, Hampton, Carter, Bridger, Leroy, Hilliard, Aspen, Alcova, Mormon Town, Bracket (Brackett) City, Maysville, Tubb Town,[174] Dwyer, Uva, Teapot, Trabing, Bingham, Wolton, Fence, Cactus, Lost, Anchor, Salt Springs, Circle, Bedlam, Frederick, Reshaw, Blazon, Wyotah, Emigh, Akwenasa, Raven, Poposie, Pacific Springs, Badwater, Dumbell, Camp Stool, Vonnie, Underwood, Metzler, Labonte, Gallio, Pleasel, Brase, Tipperary, Verse, Punteney, Bonnide, Bishop, Lindbergh, Inyankara, Poor, and Black Butler.

Military sites include Forts MacKenzie, Phil Kearney, McKinney, Reno (Connor), Bernard, Casper, Fetterman, Laramie, Platte, Warren, La Clede, Sanders, Halleck, Washakie (New Camp Brown), Augur (Old Camp Brown), McGraw (Thompson), Stambaugh, Steele, Supply, Piney, Warren (D. A. Russell, Camp Carlin), and Bridger; Camps Sulphur Creek, Scott, Pilot Butte, Marshall, O. O. Howard, Walbach, and Butter Cottonwood; and the Reno Cantonment.

Some camps were "end of track" for railroad construction crews, here today, gone tomorrow, as the shining, serpentine steel tracks were relentlessly pushed west. For a while the workers and camp followers added to the strident cacaphony of camp life. It was a tough life for tough people, including the women—who were frequently as tough as hickory and hard as bull quartz.[175]

Ephemeral stage and pony express stations dotted the state—fleeting and illusory as shadows. They included Jenny and Beaver Stockades, Canyon Springs, Cheyenne River, Robber's Roost, May's, Old Woman, Hat Creek, Harding, Running Water, Silver Springs, Rawhide Butte, Government Farm, 10 Mile, Sand Point, 3 Mile Ranch, Eagle's Nest, Rock Ranch, Gold Springs, Chug Springs, Bordeaux, Chimney Rock, Chugwater, Bear Springs, Little Bear, Horse Creek, Pole Creek, 9 Mile, Willow Springs, Big Laramie, La Prele, Moss Agate, Point of Rocks, 40 Mile, 22 Mile, Little Laramie, Cooper Creek, Rock Creek, Medicine Bow, Elk Mountain, Pass Creek, Midway, North Platte, Sage Creek, Pine Grove, Bridger Pass, Sulphur Springs, Soldier's Wells, Muddy Bridge, Duck Lake, Buffalo Wallow, Cook's 17 Mile, Red Butte, Willow Springs, Horse Creek, Sweetwater, Devil's Gate, Plant's, Split Rock, Three Crossing, Elkhorn, Ice Springs, Myersville, Hailey, Derby, Burnt Ranch, Pacific Springs, McCann Ranch, Dry Sandy, Little Sandy, Big Sandy, Big Timber, Green River, Martin's, Alkali, Ham's Fork, Church Butte, Millersville, Quaking Asp Springs, Barrel Springs, Big Pond, Black Butte, Crook's Gap, Bull Springs, Bell Springs, Antelope Creek, Sand Creek, Brown Springs, Sage Creek, and Lost Soldier.

Bullwhackers, honyockers, whores, gamblers, saloon keepers, blacksmiths, cowpunchers, sheepmen, gandy dancers, miners, soldiers, prospectors, all made Wyoming history. And if little remains physically, everyone is poorer because of it.

But enough lives on in Big, Wonderful Wyoming that reflects much of the good and bad, the strong and the weak, the admirable and the contemptible. Many camps died a-bornin', but some have tenaciously hung on and survive today. Here today, they may be gone tomorrow. But live or dead, healthy or ailing, lively or comatose, much of the lusty, brawling, occasionally halcyon past is still visible, or can be imagined traveling the avenues of dusty death through *Wyoming* ghost towns and mining camps.

What remains of Fort Stambaugh

A motel near Aladdin

Some crumbling remains at Sage

The inscription reads, "Robert Widdowfield. Erected by his Friends. Murdered near Elk Mountain, August 19, 1878. Aged 33 years." The popular peace officer was ambushed by outlaws.

Notes

1. Paul is correct as far as gold and silver mining are concerned. There has been very little silver mined in Wyoming. The total gold output for the state has been slightly over 82,000 ounces. See *Principal Gold-Producing Districts of the United States*, U.S. Geological Survey Professional Paper 610, A. H. Koschmann and M. H. Bergendahl, U.S. Government Printing Office, Washington, D.C., 1968, p. 262.

2. C. G. Coutant, *History of Wyoming*, Chaplin, Spafford and Mathison, Laramie, 1899, p. 658.

3. Feb. 9, 1915.

4. Mary Lou Pence and Lola M. Homsher, *The Ghost Towns of Wyoming*, Hastings House, New York, 1956, p. 206.

5. Robert P. Fuller, *Wonderful Wyoming*, State Board of Immigration, Cheyenne, 1911, p. 79.

6. Cleo Christiansen, *Sagebrush Settlements*, Mountain States Printing, Lovell, Wyoming, 1967, p. 12.

7. Fuller, p. 79.

8. Prairie Publishing Co., Casper, 1936, p. 138.

9. The U.S. Bureau of Mines Bulletin 586, *Historical Summary of Coal-Mine Explosions in the United States, 1810-1958*, U.S. Government Printing Office, Washington, D.C., 1960, (and several other sources), indicate that there was a March 4, 1881 fire at Almy (the state's first), which claimed 38 lives (35 Chinese and 3 Whites), and a fire in 1886 claimed the lives of 11 men and 2 boys. "History" is probably wrong, for it is commonly held that a total of three mine fires—(in 1881, 1886, and 1895)—took 87 lives. However, an exhaustive study of available data indicates that the only mine fire in Wyoming between the 1886 fire at Almy and the March 28, 1908 fire at Hanna was a conflagration at Red Canyon, March 20, 1895, which killed 62 persons.

10. Velma Linford, *Wyoming Frontier State*, Old West Publishing Company, Denver, Colorado, 1947, p. 273, gives the 32 year figure, but the mines apparently operated from 1881 to 1905 or 1906.

11. *Ibid*.

12. For more detials on related race riots, see the section on Rock Springs.

13. The Laramie *Boomerang* of Feb. 13, 1906, indicates, "Mine No. 5 at Almy which has been a hoodoo colliery for twenty years, has at last been formally abandoned. The dollar per ton mining figure is given in *History of the Union Pacific Coal Mines*, no author given, Union Pacific Coal Co., Colonial Press, Lincoln, Nebraska, 1940, p. 100.

14. Mae Urbanek, *Wyoming Wonderland*, Sage Books, Denver, 1964, p. 52.

15. Norman Weis, in *Ghost Towns of the Northwest*, Caxton, Caldwell, Idaho, 1971, p. 193 gives the date as 1862, clearly in error.

16. State of Wyoming Historical Department, *Bulletin*, Cheyenne, July 15, 1924, Vol. 2, No. 1, p. 7.

17. Muriel Sibell Wolle, *The Bonanza Trail*, Indiana University Press, Bloomington, 1953, p. 169.

18. The Sheridan *Press*, Sheridan, July 17, 1963.

19. Pence and Homsher, p. 177

20. Linford says it was one-half million; Pence and Homsher estimate the figure at two million. It is not clear if the "amalgamator" was the Kirschener-Washington stamp mill, as reported in the Sheridan *Enterprise* June 20, 1896.

21. Wolle, p. 156

22. Pence & Homsher, pp. 132-33.

23. Wolle, p. 157.

24. Pence & Homsher, p. 133. Lambert Florin, in *Ghost Town Album*, Superior, Seattle, 1962, p. 160, gives a slightly different version.

25. Alexander Toponce, in *Reminiscences of Alexander Toponce*, University of Oklahoma Press, Norman, 1971, p. 142, claims it was he who went to the rear of the newspaper tent, just as the crowd approached the front and slit the tent with his knife and got the editor on a mule, making good his escape; Legh Freeman and his brother-partner Fred claimed the Union Pacific had a hand in the newspaper office destruction. The brothers contended the railroad had "jumped" their coal mine claim and accused the UP of illegal seizure. They were convinced the railroad had helped put them out of business to silence any campaign of protest by the *Index*.

26. Probably editor Legh Freeman.

27. Saratoga *Sun*, Nov. 17, 1938.

28. Walker, p. 137.

29. Lambert Florin, in *Western Ghost Towns*, Superior, Seattle, 1964, p. 166, indicates that anthracite coal was also found at Glencoe, Wyoming. There is no confirmation of this.

30. According to Watson Parker and Hugh Lambert in *Black Hills Ghost Towns*, Sage Books, Chicago, 1974, p. 54, coal deposits were first discovered in the area in Coal Creek Canyon in 1887 by Frank Mondell.

31. Pence and Homsher, p. 162.

32. Urbanek, p. 72.

33. Urbanek indicates that even table dishes were owned by the company.

34. Pence and Homsher estimate 550 (p. 162), as do Parker and Lambert (p. 55).

35. Estimates of the total number of ovens range from 24 to 74.

36. Ethelbert Talbot, *My People of the Plains*, Harper and Brothers, New York, 1906, p. 170.

37. Mabel Brown and Elizabeth Thorpe, *...And Then There Was One*, privately published, Newcastle, Wyoming, 1965, p. 3.

38. *History of the Union Pacific Coal Mines*, p. 28.

39. Pence and Homsher, p. 66, say there were seven. In *Wyoming*, American Guide Series, Writers' Program of the W.P.A., Oxford University Press, New York, 1941, the figure given is six.

40. W. F. Rae, *Westward by Rail*, Promontory Press, New York (originally published by D. Appleton & Company, New York, 1871), 1974, p. 92.

41. Pence and Homsher, p. 65.

42. *Annals of Wyoming*, Vol. 8, No. 4, April, 1932, p. 634.

43. Sometimes "sprag poles" were used—poles originally designed to support roofs of underground mine tunnels. See *The River of Green and Gold*, by Fred W. Rabe and David C. Flaherty, Idaho Research Foundation, Moscow, 1974, p. 20. Charles Howard Shinn, in *The Story of the Mine*, D. Appleton and Company, New York, 1896, p. 236, calls them "spraggs," and claims the wooden sticks are six or eight inches long.

44. The gang probably included, among others, Joe Manuse, Frank James, John Irwin, and Frank Towle.

45. Big Nose George Parrot was caught a couple of years later at Rawlins, forced to climb a ladder which was set up against a lamp post, and told to jump. The rope broke, and the angry crowd shot him to death. Rumors persist that the Union Pacific had a Rawlins mortician skin "Big Nose" to make moccasins and other "memorabilia" for the railroad. Other versions have it that the body was given to Dr. John E. Osborne, who used it for anatomical study. Osborne also reportedly made trimming for his medical kit from skin from Parrott's chest, and a pair of shoes from Parrott's thighs. Some say he even sawed off the top of Big Nose's skull and it was used for a doorstop (See Robert Karolevitz, *Doctors of the Old West*, Bonanza Books, New York, 1967, p. 109).

46. Rawlins *Daily Times*, August 23, 1949.

47. Carbon is not to be confused with "Carbon Timber Town," on the east bank of the North Platte River near Fort Fred Steele. See Norman Weis, *Ghost Towns of the Northwest*, pp. 227-38.

48. T. A. Larson, *History of Wyoming*, University of Nebraska Press, 1965, p. 134 says the Centennial District opened in 1876, but two years later had petered out.

49. *Wyoming*, p. 256.

50. Christiansen, p. 22.

51. Possibly, at one time, at least, the camp was known as Copper Hill, since it was a copper mining camp.

52. Christiansen, p. 23.

53. Fuller, p. 89 says 2,500; the 1920 *Wyoming State Directory* agrees; Linford says 3,000.

54. Union Pacific History, p. 133.

55. *Ibid.*

56. Homsher and Pence say it was 1930, so does the Union Pacific History; Linford gives 1929 as the closing date.

57. Roughly Scandinavian for "a crown."

58. Pence and Homsher, p. 209.

59. Laramie *Boomerang*, Feb. 19, 1901.

60. *Ibid.*, Feb. 8, 1901.

61. *Ibid.*, Jan. 20, 1900.

62. St. Paul *Pioneer Press*, Feb. 2, 1901.

63. Pence and Homsher, p. 206.

64. Larson, pp. 305-6.

65. Pence and Homsher, p. 206.

66. Fuller, p. 93.

67. They were worked by Thomas Sneddon.

68. Bureau of Mines *Bulletin* 586, p. 22.

69. The Missoula (Montana) *Missoulian*, May 19, 1973, gives the larger figure. The 1920 through 1929 *Wyoming State Business Directory* lists the smaller figure.

70. Sheridan *Post*, Aug. 9, 1903.

71. *Ibid.*

72. Fuller, p. 95.

73. *Wyoming* says his first name was "Millica" (p. 123).

74. Pence and Homsher, p. 123.

75. *Ibid.*

76. Alfred J. Mokler, *History of Natrona County Wyoming*, Argonaut Press, New York, 1966, p. 230.

77. Pence and Homsher give this figure, on p. 214. Newspaper accounts of the day seem not to credit more than 3,000 to 4,000 people in the area.

78. Mokler, p. 230.

79. The U.S. Department of the Interior National Park Service publication, *Prospector, Cowhand, and Sodbuster*, 1967, p. 259 says the year was 1899. A sign at the smelter site gives the date as 1901. Pence and Homsher, p. 143 write: "In 1900 the Godsell Custom smelter was erected." The Laramie *Boomerang* of August 21, 1901 states that "The Boston-Wyoming Company's plant—the only smelter in the state will be 'blown in' soon."

80. Pence and Homsher, p. 143.

81. *Prospector, Cowhand, and Sodbuster* says it was in 1905.

82. Pence and Homsher, p. 143.

83. Wolle, p. 155.

84. Pence and Homsher, p. 143.

85. *Ibid.*

86. Wolle, p. 155.

87. Pence and Homsher, p. 143.

88. *Wyoming*, p. 258.

89. Christiansen, p. 35.

90. Walker, p. 261.

91. Walker, p. 262.

92. Lambert Florin, *Western Ghost Towns*, Superior Publishing Company, Seattle, 1964, p. 167.

93. *Ibid.*, p. 168.

94. *Wyoming*, p. 281.

95. *Ibid.*

96. *Ibid.*

97. Saratoga *Sun*, April 10, 1896.

98. A short-lived mining camp named Herman was located near Gold Hill.

99. Saratoga *Sun*, May 3, 1894.

100. Christiansen, p. 43.

101. Wolle, p. 169 says it was a 10-stamp mill; Pence and Homsher opt for a six-stamp mill (p. 48).

102. Wolle says that the amount was recovered during the first half year of operation (p. 169); but Weis, p. 210, says that it was a full years' operation.

103. Weis, p. 210.

104. *Ibid.*, p. 207.

105. Robert A. Murray, *Miner's Delight, Investor's Despair*, Piney Creek Press, Sheridan, Wyoming, 1972, p. 28.

106. James Chisholm, *South Pass, 1868*, (edited by Lola Homsher), University of Nebraska Press, Lincoln, 1960, p. 89.

107. *Ibid.*, p. 91.

108. Chisholm, p. 90.

109. *Ibid.*, p. 104.

110. *Ibid.*, p. 105.

111. Linford, p. 355.

112. Linford says it was 169, as does the *Union Pacific History*. Larson, p. 337, gives the figure as 171.

113. Linford indicates that a second explosion caved in the mine, and that a third trapped 41 members of the rescue team. The *Union Pacific History* indicates total lives lost at 59. Bureau of Mines *Bulletin* 586 agrees with the figure of 59.

114. Larson, p. 338.

115. Christiansen, p. 47.

116. W.P.A. files, Wyoming State Historical Department.

117. Dorothy M. Johnson, in *Western Badmen*, Dodd, Mead, New York, 1970, p. 212, gives his age as 14. Christiansen, p. 48, puts the age at 13.

118. Wyoming *Eagle*, June 3, 1955.

119. Cody *Enterprise*, Dec. 3, 1969.

120. Weis, p. 217.

121. A.B. Ostrander, *After 60 years*, Gateway Printing Company, Seattle, 1925, p. 41.

122. Christiansen, p. 68.

123. Sheridan *Press*, Oct. 21, 1953.

124. An article in the (Missoula, Montana) *Missoulian*, May 19, 1973, gives a population figure of 2,000.

125. Barry B. Combs, in *Westward to Promontory*, American West Publishing Company, Palo Alto, California, 1969, p. 27, perhaps correctly suggests Durant's primary concern in building the U.P. was for quick profits.

126. Now the Southern Pacific railroad.

127. Buffalo *Bulletin*, Aug. 15, 1957.

128. William A. Baillie-Grohman, *Camps in the Rockies*, Charles Scribner's Sons, New York, 1882 (and 1910) p. 197.

129. *Ibid.*

130. Encampment *Echo*, Nov. 2, 1939.

131. Pence and Homsher, p. 142.

132. *Ibid.*

133. Some sources place the number of Chinese massacred at 28.

134. Urbanek, p. 71.

135. Christiansen, p. 83.

136. Laramie *Boomerang,* Sept. 1, 1901.

137. *Ibid.*

138. Urbanek, p. 88.

139. Pence and Homsher, p. 118.

140. *Ibid.,* p. 120.

141. The (Missoula, Montana) *Missoulian,* May 19, 1973.

142. Much information on Kooi was obtained from Doris Kooi Reynolds of Sheridan, daughter of Peter Kooi.

143. Personal interview with Stan Kuzara of Sheridan, son of the founder of Kuzaraville.

144. Wyoming silver mining is not even mentioned in the rather exhaustive book by T. H. Watkins, *Gold and Silver in the West,* American West Publishing Company, Palo Alto, 1971.

145. She was called "Old Mother Feather Legs" because she wore red drawers which were visible, flapping in the wind, as she rode her horse. Vardis Fisher, in *Gold Rushes and Mining Camps of the Early American West,* Caxton, Caldwell, 1968, p. 394, calls her Madame Featherlegs.

146. Booze was called by many names. British sportsman Baillie-Grohman said of tangleleg that cowboys said that "one drink of it tempts you to steal your own clothes, two drinks makes you bite off your own ears, while three will actually make you save your drowning mother-in-law."

147. Coutant, p. 640.

148. Pence and Homsher, p. 30.

149. Wolle, p. 162.

150. Pence and Homsher say he was "in uniform with the Nevada Volunteers," (p. 30). Wolle claims Ryan was with a detachment of troops from Fort Bridger (p. 162).

151. Rossiter W. Raymond, *Statistics of Mines and Mining in the States and Territories West of the Rocky Mountains,* 2nd report: U.S. 41st Congress, 2nd session, H.R. 207, 1870, pp. 327-8 spells the name of the lode "Cariso."

152. Weis, p. 198 and Urbanek, p. 51, say 2,000.

153. *Prospector, Cowhand, and Sodbuster,* p. 172, and Wolle, p. 163, give the 400 figure. Robert Silverberg, in *Ghost Towns of the American West,* Thomas Y. Crowell, New York, 1968, p. 200, agrees with the 4,000 figure.

154. Wolle, p. 165, says it was the *second* largest city.

155. Chisholm, p. 61.

156. *Ibid.,* p. 160.

157. Larson, p. 209.

158. Pence and Homsher, p. 39.

159. Chisholm, p. 41.

160. *Ibid.,* pp. 102-3.

161. See Cora M. Beach, *Women of Wyoming,* Casper, 1927, p. 12 for this account.

162. Whether or not Bright was at the "tea party," it appears that Mrs. Morris worked more through Mrs. Bright than through the colonel in her suffrage efforts (see the "Wyoming Tea Party" chapter in Dee Brown's *The Gentle Tamers*, Barrie and Jenkins, London, 1973).

163. Wolle (p. 165) says there were 40 cases tried. Pence and Homsher (p. 35) place the figure at 34. Todd Webb, in *Gold Strikes and Ghost Towns*, Doubleday, Garden City, (p. 142) says she tried 70 cases.

164. Chisholm, p. 63.

165. The August 18th *Frontier Index* said most people had moved to Green River City to work on railroad construction crews.

166. Chisholm, pp. 73-4.

167. Agnes Wright Spring in *The Cheyenne and Black Hills Stage and Express Routes*, University of Nebraska Press, Lincoln, 1948, p. 354, using Brown's "Gazeteer of the Union Pacific railroad, 1869," tells of the Union Pacific using coal from "Thorp, Head & Street's mine," purchased December 3, 1868. The source continued "Mr. Russell Thorp discovered these two veins of coal as early as the spring of 1868."

168. U.S. Geological Survey *Bulletin* 586, p. 100.

169. According to Linford, p. 366, the town was incorporated in 1916.

170. Christiansen, p. 93.

171. Urbanek, p. 87.

172. *Union Pacific History*, p. 108.

173. Weis makes this claim on p. 238.

174. In *The Old Timer's Tale*, El Comancho, (n.a.) The Canterbury Press, Chicago, 1929, p. 32, there is mention of "Whoop-Up Town," near Tubb Town, called "Tubtown" in that publication.

175. A phrase used in *Reminiscences of Alexander Toponce, Written by Himself*, University of Oklahoma Press, Norman, 1971 edition, p. 210.

Index

Acme, 76, *76*, 77, 78
Aderville, 3
Afton, 3, *3*
Aladdin, 4, *101*
Alamo, 4
Almy, 4, 86
Altamont. *See* Gold Hill
Antelope City. *See* Cambria
Arland's, 4
Atlantic City, 4-5, *5*, *6*, *7*, 43

Bairoil, 8
Baker Town, 4
Bald Mountain City, 8, *8*, *9*
Baldy City. *See* Bald Mountain City
Barret, Town, 4
Battle, 10-11, *10*, *11*
Bear River City, 12, *12*
Beartown. *See* Bear River City
Birdseye, 13
Blairstown, 13
Bonanza, 13
Bon Rico, 40

Calpet, 13
Cambria, 13-14, *14*, *15*, 40
Camp Muddy. *See* Cumberland
Carbon, 16-18, *16-17*, *18*, *19*, *20*, 31
Carney. *See* Carneyville
Carneyville. 77. *See also* Kleenburn
Centennial, 21, *21*, 52
City of Broken Hearts. *See* Bald Mountain City
Clearmont, 22
Coalmont, 22
Cokeville, 22, *22*, *23*
Columbine, 23
Cooper Hill, 23
Copperopolis, 23
Copperton, 24, *24*
Cora, 24
Crosby, 40
Cumberland, 4, 25, *25*, *26*, *27*, *28*, *29*, *30*
Cummins City, 31

Dana, 31
Diamondville, 31-32, *32*, 40, 64
Dietz, 33, *33*, *34*
Dillon, 35, *35*
Doggett. *See* Riverside

Eadsville, 36
Elk Mountain, *102*
Elwood, 36
Encampment, 36-37, *36*, *37*, *38*, *39*, 71, 99

Fairbanks, 40
Fort Stambaugh, *101*
Fortunatus. *See* Bald Mountain City
Frontier, 40

Gebo, 40
Gilmer, *See* Bear River City
Glencoe, 40-41
Glenrock, 41
Gold City. *See* Gold Hill
Golden Courier. *See* Gold Hill
Gold Hill, 41-42, *41*, *42*
Grand Encampment. *See* Encampment
Grass Creek, 43
Greenville. *See* Gold Hill
Guernsey, 40, 43, 50, 57
Gunn, 43

Hamilton City, 43
Hanna, 18, 46, *46*, *47*, *48*, *49*, 86
Hartville, 50, *50*, *51*, 87
Hecla, 52
Home Camp. *See* Midwest
Hotchkiss, 77

Iron Mountain, 52
Irontown. *See* Upton

Jelm. *See* Cummins City
Johnstown, 52

Keystone, 52, *52*
Kirby, 40
Kirwin, 52
Kleenburn, 77, *77*, *78*. *See also* Carneyville
Kooi, 78
Kuzaraville, 78

Lamont, 52
La Plata, 41
Lavoye, 53, *53*
Leadville, 54
Leslie, 54
Lewiston, 54, *54*, *55*, *56*, 57
Lusk, 57, 79. *See also* Silver Cliff
Lysite, 52

McFadden, 57
Manville, 57
Megeath. *See* Winton
Mercedes. *See* Glenrock
Merino. *See* Upton
Midwest, 57
Millerburg, 57
Mineral Hill, 58, *58*, 59
Miner's Delight, 43-44, *43*, *44*, *45*
Model, 78
Monarch, 60, *61*, *62*, *63*, 77, 78, *78*

New Rochelle, *See* Silver Cliff
Nuttall. *See* Glenrock

Oakley, 64
Old Baldy. *See* Bald Mountain City
Old Gold City. *See* Bald Mountain City

Parco, 64, *64*
Peckville, 57
Piedmont, 65, *65*, *66*, *67*, 68
Platinum City, 68

Ragtown, 68
Rambler, 69, *69*, 70
Red Canyon, 70
Reliance. *See:* Cumberland; Superior
Richieville, 70
Riverside, 71, *71*, *72*
Rock Springs, 73, *73*
Rudefeha, 35, 37, 68, 74, *73*, *75*
Running Water. *See* Silver Cliff

Sage, *102*
Savery, 74
Sheridan: more ghost towns in area of, 76-78, *76*, *77*, *78*
Silver City. *See* Silver Crown
Silver Cliff, 79
Silver Crown, 79
Sinclair, 64, *64*. *See also* Parco
Slack, 86, *86*
Smith's Fork. *See* Cokeville
South Pass City, 1, 4, 43, 79-82, *80*, *81*, *82*, *83*, *84*, *85*
Spring Valley, 4, 86
Sublett (Sublet, Sublette), 87
Sunrise, 87, *87*, *88*
Superior, 89, *89*, *90*, *91*, *92*, *93*, *94*, *95*, *96*, *97*
Sweetwater, 5, 98. *See also* Atlantic City

Tie Siding, 98, *98*
Twin Creeks, 99

Upton, 99

Walcott, 99
Welcome, 59, 60, *60*
Winton, 99

Afterword, 100: list of additional ghost towns, other than mining camps